MOURNING N

Bob Will

INTRODUCTION

"A MOURNING MOMENT" articles were born from the desire to normalize grief emotions and provide some guidance to hurting hearts. The acceptance of the content confirmed a need for simple, direct, and sensitive grief education. There is a need for "tools", or a guide, to help affirm the journey through grief.

The "tools' provided in this material have been shared in grief support groups, workshops, and grief seminars across the country. They are valuable...when applied.

This book can be a "tool". Write in this book. Write your feelings into the margins, at the end of chapters, even add pages if you need to. Let this book be a guide, a journal, and a safe place for expressing emotions, thoughts, and feelings.

The articles chosen for this book are a portion shared with grievers around the world. I believe the true heroes in grief are those who continue to put one foot in front of the other in their heart-wrenching journey each day.

I wish the very best for each of you in all things.

Blessings,

Bob Willis

CONTENTS

GIVING and RECEIVING SUPPORT

EXPRESSING EMOTIONS

TOOLS

HOLIDAYS

GIVING and
RECEIVING SUPPORT

TAKE TIME TO NOTICE

I sat in a doctor's waiting room, "waiting" my turn. As usual, I was casually doing my public hobby of "watching people". We can learn a lot by just observing the activity around us.

Across the room there was a young mother with her toddler. I noticed the toddler was very active, but still not in complete control of legs and balance. So, with his mother holding his arms, he was able to walk across the room. It was not a pretty walk, but he got from Point A to Point B, with his mother providing his balance.

Then I saw the other extreme. Into the waiting area walked an elderly couple. Obvious physical challenges had left the elderly man with difficulty walking. Each step seemed to be a challenge, but he was not giving up or complaining. His dear wife was doing what the toddler's mother was doing...she held his arms to provide security and balance until he was safely resting in a chair.

Mothers, wives, husbands, children, other family members and even strangers can provide support for us at times. Naturally we expect toddlers to need support, and someone is usually quick to respond. But what about another adult? Are we quick to offer support and security to another adult in need?

We see the need for physical support often, but how aware are we of the need for emotional support? Let's try this, in a public setting when we notice someone who appears to be having a difficult day...let's lay a smile and kind word onto them. Look for a light in their eyes, or a smile on their face, just because someone took time to encourage, acknowledge, and cover them with kindness.

It can make a difference...for all of us.

WHEN GIVERS NEED HELP

He had always been the first one to step up and help others in their time of need. Now he was in bed, recovering from illness, and there was work which needed to be done. His son-in-law recruited many of us to complete the work necessary in the field so the "crop was in the barn" on time.

Before we left his home, I stepped in to visit with him. He was in bed, tears filled his eyes, and he said "I have always been the helper, it is very hard to be helped". Love was poured upon this man and his sweet family on that day...well deserved. It changed all of us.

Sometimes, we are called to be the "giver", meeting needs for someone else. It just feels right to help each other, encourage each other, and support someone else in their time of need. But things can change in an instant due to sickness, or even a death.

Perhaps we have been guilty of saying it to someone in grief, "If you need anything, just call me". Sounds great, but not very realistic. People seldom call if they need something, maybe out of pride, maybe embarrassed, there can be many reasons NOT to call for help.

Instead of waiting for that call, perhaps we should step up first. Because of our own experience at a time of loss, we have insight into what will help most.

We know what will be supportive…why wait for a phone call? What did someone do for you that helped? As much as we can, let's refrain from "if you need anything, just call me". Perhaps God is already making the call to us.

4-LETTER WORDS

"D**N". I heard my dad say that word one time. My oldest sister also heard it another time. Both occasions were times of sudden pain for him. We were not raised in a home that used "4-letter words". Now they seem to be normal and accepted in society.

Of course, there are some "4-letter words" to describe the process of dealing with grief. These are very common words and feelings. In fact, until we acknowledge and identify with these words, we will not see our need to mourn.

LOSS...HURT...PAIN...GONE...NEED...FEAR.

But there are some helpful and necessary "4-letter words" to be used around grievers.

CARE...HELP...LOVE...TALK...HOPE...CALM.

Instead of feeling hopeless and helpless around those in grief, perhaps we can look for ways to insert "4-letter words" into their life. In the midst of their darkness and sorrow, let's try to insert some light through our presence and support.

We cannot "fix" a griever. They need the support from someone willing to share and use "4-letter words".

Will you be that "someone"?

BEING INTENTIONALLY KIND

The phrase "practice random kindness and senseless acts of beauty" was written by Anne Herbert on a placemat in Sausalito, CA, in 1982. (Wikipedia)

When we practice random acts of kindness, it releases positive vibes. We feel better and the recipients feel better, which makes them more likely to be kind to others.

Do you want to make a difference in a life today? You can, we all can, IF we want to.

The emotions of grief can paralyze us and steal our motivation. Each person is faced with a choice to quit, give up, or continue moving ahead in the grief journey. Giving up is a big temptation to many, but not the best choice for anyone.

But what if we intentionally honored our loved one with random acts of KINDNESS? Or CARING? Or COMPASSION? It may involve nothing more than a smile, a short conversation, a compliment, a helping hand, a few dollars, or a few minutes of our time.

Let's look for the opportunity to make a difference in a life today. As you are doing this, imagine your loved one smiling at you...because you are making someone's life a little easier.

MAKING EYE CONTACT

It is something I must force myself to do. It does not come natural for me. I speak to crowds, groups, and individuals, but this is something I must intentionally do. I try to make eye contact with someone. Not everyone is comfortable with eye contact. It is more difficult than you think.

Social media is a tremendous avenue to communicate words, but we cannot fully express true feelings through just words. Meeting face to face cannot be replaced through photos or videos.

Recently I read that eye contact is usually 3.2 seconds with a stranger. With family or friends eye contact can be much longer.

We may look toward someone as we talk, but do we actually make eye contact with them? Making eye contact can allow us to build a comfort level and accept/reject what is being said. Think about it.

Do you notice eye colors? The eye color of your loved one is probably deeply engrained into your memory. You would notice right away if you saw someone with a similar eye color. That is special.

Remember, we lose the physical relationship. Emotionally and spiritually we never lose anyone...a gift to be treasured.

ASSEMBLY LINE OF LIFE

My wife does not sew, and that is OK with me. While I was a ministry student, she worked to provide additional income for our family.

Her job? Sewing the fly onto jeans in a factory. That was her contribution to provide a final product...she sewed the fly onto the jeans. This is a very important piece, perhaps THE most important.

It was an assembly line production. Everyone was expected to do their part. There were quotas and pressure to produce. If even 1 person lagged behind, it impacted the entire process.

Isn't life like that? Everyone has a role, a purpose, something to contribute to life. If even 1 person is taken from the circle, if death occurs and there is an empty place, it impacts everyone. Our vision for what life should look like can change immediately. The dream we had can disappear because someone is missing. Our hopes can be destroyed by a single telephone call. Life can change suddenly and the pain can be indescribable.

After a loss we are on another assembly line. We can only take care of our part, we can only be responsible for our task. It is important to take care of ourselves physically, emotionally, and spiritually. We must concentrate on our part.

Perhaps we cannot see the final product yet, but each part is very important. Do not quit! Do not give up! Each little part is needed and important for the finished product.

MEN AND WOMEN ARE DIFFERENT

It was obvious to me again today...men and women are different. Some differences are more obvious than others, lol. I go into the store to BUY and item...my wife goes into the store to SHOP...there IS a big difference. Men like to get in, get it, and get out. Women tend to see everything and touch most things...haahaa.

In the area of grief there are also differences. Women are usually more emotional, outwardly expressing feelings. Men tend to hold emotions on the inside, not quick to open up and share their grief.

Expressing grief as a male or female does not decide if it is right or wrong. Learning to express grief outwardly can be healthy physically and emotionally.

Common behaviors or signs of grief for men can include:

- Keeping to themselves; dealing with it silently without strong outward feelings
- Control; men may fear that expressing feelings is a sign of weakness
- Fix-it; a problem solving mode, focused on projects and control

Women may express grief by:

- Telling their story; the more it is told the more they feel heard and supported
- Seek support; finding a safe outlet for expressing grief is important
- Remembrance; a need to honor lives and tell stories

Male or female, if you have experienced a loss, be open and honest with your emotions. Seek the support of a professional, or a grief support group. Reaching out for help is NOT a sign of weakness, rather it is a sign of making a mature and helpful decision.

FIND YOUR GUIDE

Yes, I do some strange things. I'm aware of that, and my family can attest to that fact. But hey, life should be interesting...right?

We have lived in our home almost 25 years. I'm very comfortable in my environment. So, occasionally I close my eyes and imagine what it would be like to have no sight. I know the number of steps from my bed to the bedroom doorknob, I know where to reach for the light switch, I even know how many steps it takes to get to a chair. There is a comfort level because I am familiar with my surroundings.

But, what about a strange environment. I would be a fool to try walking with my eyes closed in a different area. I would be fearful to take a step, not knowing what was ahead of me. Each step would be a risk for falling. It would help if someone was nearby to say "one more small step....you will have a small step downward...now you can reach out and touch the chair".

The presence and guiding voice of a trusted friend can be helpful in areas in which we are not familiar. Often we need the assurance when someone says "You are doing the right thing", or "sit and relax a few minutes", or "this can be risky, so let's be careful and take our time".

It can be helpful to have a calming presence alongside us in the grief journey. A trusted friend can help recognize pit falls and areas of conflict we may not be aware of. They can also be a sounding board to express feelings and discuss necessary decisions that must be made.

Find your guide, trust their insight and experience. This takes trust…but we need this trust in the uncharted territory called grief.

A SMILE IN ANY LANGUAGE

"Everyone smiles in the same language" (George Carlin)

George Carlin was an American comedian whose caustic style of humor caused us to look closely at society. Most of his material cannot be shared in mixed company, but the quote above is true and accurate.

Technology today will allow us to connect with people from around the world, night or day, seven days a week. We can be exposed to different cultures, different religions, and different languages…all within the confines of our own home. We can "travel the world" without leaving our comfortable chair.

I've noticed that death is also universal, but the expressions of mourning are different around the world. Some cultures honor deceased loved ones on a regular basis, and their grief is part of life. Others attempt to put the death and grief emotions behind them and make efforts to begin a fresh life. Tears and pain are also universal.

As Carlin mentioned, each language and culture will understand a smile. Acknowledging another person with a smile, even making eye contact when allowed and appropriate, is a sign of respecting and welcoming another person. Smiles can be contagious…just give someone your smile and watch for it to be reflected back at you.

Smiles are the universal language…we need to speak that language often and teach it to others.

CATCH A FALLING STAR

"Catch A Falling Star". That was a new sign outside our daughter's hospital room. She had a fall when away from her bed, so the nurses stepped up awareness that she was a high fall risk. No damage done, but now she is referred to as a "Falling Star".

It would be helpful if we had signs we could display or wording on a shirt, that says "Catch A Falling Star". This could be especially helpful following a loss, because grievers will fall quite often.

The "Falling Star" portion can refer to a griever who is very normal in their responses to loss. It can refer to the emotional roller coaster that can produce sudden outbursts of memories and tears. It can also refer to a griever who seems to be doing well, but a memory can be overwhelming. When those emotions sneak up on a griever, it is quite common and normal to "fall" into a pile of tears.

In fact, it may be helpful to inform family and friends that you may become a "falling star" at any moment. As this occurs, we need someone who will "catch us", someone who will understand our need to express emotions. Others can "catch us" by giving us time and space, and by listening when we need to share feelings. Do not apologize for being a "Falling Star". It is part of the process of finding our strength and balance.

DOWN THE ROAD

Have you ever used the phrase "down the road"? I've heard this all my life. It is used for talking about the future and what may (or may not) happen. A lot of things can happen..."down the road".

"Down the road" there can be many curves. In most cases there will be signs giving the direction the curve will take, and a suggested safe speed to continue around the curve. Life will throw us some curves, we do not always see the direction they will take, and we must quickly adjust our speed to prevent a disaster. It helps to slow down.

"Down the road" can bring about decisions...forks in the road. When faced with decisions it is good to consider the options and think through the end result of each choice. Often it is helpful to talk with someone who has been "down the road" before and get their insight on how to make the journey safer. They may know of obstacles to be overcome and areas in which to be more cautious.

"Down the road" is the direction all of us are traveling. It can be frightening to be a griever because the journey is a new experience for us. Be aware of the safest speed for you, be aware of your surroundings, and do not be in a hurry.

As you are aware, you are not going "down the road" alone...many are traveling similar roads. There is a sense of uncertainty. Let's learn to rely upon others, let's watch for the curves and obstacles. We can't turn around...so let's go "down the road" together.

WINNING FRIENDS

In 1936, Dale Carnegie wrote a best selling book, "How To Win Friends and Influence People". He provided great insight into building relationships. Even today, over 85 years later, his concepts are practical and effective. Here are some of his key points:

- Be genuinely interested in others
- Smile
- Remember their name
- Be a good listener
- Talk about their interests
- Make the other person feel important

It would make a difference in lives if we could practice only 1 of these points for a week…then move down the list a week at a time. For some people these steps come easy, almost without thinking about it. For many others it becomes a struggle and it does not feel comfortable.

Was your loved one a good motivator? Were they gifted in communicating feelings? Did they make others feel special and important? There are those who are said to be a "people person", genuinely interested in others. When these people spend time with us, it makes us feel better. A "people person" is a gift to those around them.

Regardless of our life situation, we can each work on 1 of these from the list above. Who knows…it might even brighten our path when we make a difference in the life of someone else. This world needs more people who want to "win friends and influence people". Let's do it.

SELECT YOUR INNER CIRCLE

Relationships end before we are through with them. It is very common to wish for 1 more conversation, 1 more day, 1 more hug, 1 more moment to make a memory. After a death, it is common to hear someone say "it just feels so final". Yes, it is final, and the shock can be devastating.

Some well-meaning people can say some very hurtful things. I believe it is because they are not comfortable with grief, they do not know what to say, but feel obligated to say something. It can hurt when someone says "it just takes time". Yes, grief does take TIME...it takes a life-TIME. We will be grievers for the remainder of our days. It would be somewhat easier if grief did have a timeline of completion...but it does not.

Others may say "they would not want you to cry". I disagree with this statement. Crying is an outward expression of inward pain, it is our expression of grief, it is mourning. It is very healthy to mourn, that is how we find comfort with our grief. Jesus did NOT say "Blessed are those who grieve". He DID say "Blessed are those who MOURN, for they shall be comforted" (Matthew 5:4). When it comes to the emotions of grief we only have 2 choices…hold them in or let them out. It is healthier to let them out…it is mourning.

Those who meet our needs during a time of grief are the ones who allow us to share memories. They will understand when we cry, laugh, and cry some more. They will be present with our pain and not try to "fix us". They will mention the name of our loved one, even share memories of them. These are the people we need around us during our grief. This is the time to be selective who we allow into our inner circle of friends.

COMMON GROUND

"Common ground"….we can take it for granted. Being around a family structure provided "common ground" for our family. We had foods in common, activities and schedules in common, friends and common, holiday rituals in common…we shared "common ground" with family. We were comfortable with our "common ground".

After leaving home and entering the work force, or furthering our education, things can change. We will meet people who were raised differently, some with different values in life, some with stricter family rules and expectations, some with no expectations. That can be a shocking awareness.

It is quite natural to meet a stranger and begin a conversation to cover several aspects of life…trying to find "common ground" on which we can agree. Through these times of finding "common ground" we begin a relationship that can grow stronger over time.

What "common ground" did you have with your loved one who died? What common interests did you discover? Were there areas you both enjoyed that reinforced your interests? The things that are shared become "common ground", something enjoyed, something that ties the bond even tighter.

Grief support groups can have some "common ground". There are typical emotions and feelings of grief that are common for some people. There can be life and family issues since the death that form "common ground" for understanding. If we are looking for "common ground" in which to support each other, we can find it. Some people are ready to seek "common ground" with other grievers...some are not. That is OK...it is "common" to be different.

SUICIDE HELP LINE

Even if you feel lonely, you are not alone! If you are feeling lonely, reach out to an understanding loved one. If your feelings of loneliness don't go away or feel unbearable, or if you are feeling anxious or depressed, contact a mental health professional.

A good way to look at it is to ask yourself some of these questions: Are you avoiding doing things? How is your mood? Do you feel disconnected? Do you feel guilty for not talking to friends, or are you talking yourself into social situations?

All of these can be signs that you need to take steps toward developing good, intimate, and authentic relationships. Consider taking the step of making connections through a support group. Support groups address a variety of issues, from specific mental health conditions to various challenges, including grief and physical illness.

If you need help right away, contact a hotline. Dial 988, the Suicide and Crisis Lifeline. Even if you are lonely, know that you are not alone.

(The article above was taken from the McLean Harvard Medical School Affiliate article: "4 Steps to Walk Away from Loneliness" (2022).)

On a personal note...I have called 988. I refer others to call them, so I wanted to check it out. I was immediately connected with a local volunteer who provided an impressive list of resources in my community. When you need a safe person with a caring heart and helpful resources...call them...24/7...anonymous...dial 988.

THOSE WHO ACTUALLY LISTEN

"When E.F. Hutton talks, people listen" became one of the most successful advertising slogans of the late 1900's. Amid the hustle and bustle of a crowded life situation, people would talk about the stock market. When someone said "my broker is E.F. Hutton…" everyone turns to listen. The implication was that this stock firm was going to provide special insight for everyone.

Wouldn't it be helpful to have that type of attention from those around us when we wanted to talk about memories of our loved one? I believe it could benefit a griever to have the freedom to share memories, freedom to laugh or cry, and the freedom to use the name of their loved one.

When we hold the emotions of grief inside our heart and mind, it can become a very heavy load that easily slides into a deep sadness or depression. It can feel like a dark cloud in life, and it becomes heavier as time moves along. That is grief.

Mourning is the outward expression of these feelings. Mourning is "grief gone public". Everyone grieves…but not everyone mourns in healthy ways. Unhealthy ways to express the pain can involve alcohol, drugs, gambling, and relationships. It is healthier to put words to the pain of grief.

Many people say they do not have anyone who will listen to their grief. Instead of saying we do not have anyone who will listen, perhaps we should make sure we are still actively looking for that person. Observe who others share with, be selective who you share with. Intentionally build trust over time. Be open to the one who will "listen" to you…that person can be a treasure to you.

SOMEONE TO HELP US THINK

Years ago I worked for a funeral home that was keenly aware of the special needs of grievers. My role was to deliver death certificates to the home, provide a listening ear, and guide them in expressing their grief. It was a very emotional time for the family, so respect and sensitivity to their needs was of utmost importance.

This family of funeral homes had a delightful woman who provided a valuable service to families. She would sit with the family and explain all of the necessary paperwork during this difficult time. She would assist them with completing insurance paperwork.

One of the reasons this service was provided to families is because each family was in a state of shock. During this time, when grievers cannot even remember their own telephone numbers, they are called upon to remember dates, times, locations, and names.

Many refer to this as "widow brain", and there is some truth to that term. But it also impacts the family dealing with the death of a child, or another family member.

During the time of making funeral arrangements, and for years to come, we need someone to help with details when our thoughts are not complete. Because it is normal to lose focus and concentration at the time of a loss, we need a trusted support person to "help us think".

That person is a treasure, not only at the time of making arrangements, but even now in the day to day decision making. Build your support team, strengthen relationships, and trust your team. Even if it has failed in the past, or it is difficult for you to do so, it will be a very valuable decision to build your team.

BEST FRIENDS

Alan Alexander Milne (A.A. Milne), was an English author and playwright. He is best known for creating the Winnie the Pooh character, the friends of Winnie, the stories, and the quotes. For decades, Winnie the Pooh has been part of the culture around the world.

Milne's life was not without challenges and problems. Perhaps that is what led to the quotes that speak to the needs of the heart.

"A Friend is someone who helps you up when you're down, and if they can't, they lay down beside you and listen" -Winnie the Pooh.

Each one of us will face some challenges in life, and some of them will knock us down. No matter how much we try, there will be a sense of helplessness. Do not be surprised if this happens in your life, it is especially common following a death.

Yes, we need that friend who takes time to help us up, if possible. But, if they can't help us up, they do not leave or walk away. On the contrary, that special friend will lay down beside us and listen to our heart.

Those friends can be very rare. But, perhaps in order for us to HAVE ONE…we should first BE ONE. Look for the opportunity to be the type of friend that goes the extra mile in caring for

40

others. Instead of walking away, perhaps we are
expected to spend some time helping and
encouraging someone else. We will never be the
same.

LEARNING FROM OTHERS

We can all learn. In fact, there is a great opportunity to support each other in the area of grief and loss. We can share our personal knowledge of what has been valuable to us, and we can suggest steps that can be taken to soften the journey for others.

There are no magic words, there is no set pattern to confront all grief…everyone is different, so let's help each other. Perhaps you have some insight to share in these areas. Your responses can benefit many who are struggling with grief. Please share.

- How do you prepare for birthdays and holidays without your loved one?

- What is your most difficult time, and how do you make it through?

- What advice do you give someone who has just experienced the loss of a loved one?

Remember, your experience can be helpful to others. No one is on this journey alone, although it can feel lonely at times. This is a great time to give and receive support from each other.

WE DEPEND ON OTHERS

A very popular transition in the level of community living for adults is known as "Independent living". This is available to those who are still capable of caring for their own needs, are mobile, and not relying upon a caregiver.

If our child dies, the grief is difficult because we were accustomed to "Dependent Living". Our child was dependent upon our teaching of boundaries in life; dependent upon receiving discipline when necessary; dependent upon receiving guidance through life situations that are new for them; and dependent upon unconditional love. Grief can be the loss of one who was dependent upon us in life. The one we loved is no longer present for us to cover with our love and acceptance.

If our spouse/soul mate dies, we find grief to be the emptiness of someone we depended upon. We depended upon the balance that conversation gave to situations; we depended upon the emotional, Spiritual, and physical support provided by another person; We depended upon having someone we could share dreams with; we were depended upon someone who was the recipient of our unconditional love.

Because of a death, we can be forced to go from "dependent living" to "independent living". Our

43

world changes, our support systems can change, our future can be uncertain, and memories can overwhelm our emotions.

We are trying to move from "dependent living" to "independent living" and it was not our choice to do so. We would prefer to be dependent upon someone we love, and have someone to be dependent upon us. Grief leaves an emptiness and loneliness that is difficult to describe. This type of "independent living" is not what we desired.

MOURNING NOTES:

MOURNING NOTES:

<u>SELF CARE</u>

BUILDING WALLS OR BRIDGES?

"If it is different than the way I believe...then it is wrong!! If you have a different viewpoint than I have...then your viewpoint is wrong...and mine is right!"

Have you ever met anyone with that attitude? I have, and I found it very difficult to communicate with them. When a person has that attitude, it prevents them from even considering (or respecting) the viewpoint of others.

Life is too short to be spent arguing with people who have this mindset. No matter what we say or do, we will always be wrong if it does not line up with their opinions.

Grievers can be faced with these people, and it can be very hurtful. Their statements may begin with the words "Do you know what you need? Let me tell you!", or "This is what you need to do"..., or "You are doing it all wrong."

In my opinion, there are 2 types of people we confront while our grief is fresh and raw. Some people will build walls that will prevent any sharing of feelings or emotions. There will be a resistance on their part to allow conversations that might stir emotions. That is OK. Recognize it is where they are in life...and move on. Don't try to "change them" or "make it happen".

The other group will build a bridge to allow for open discussions of feelings and emotions. These people are present and supportive to grievers. Their message is "I am interested, please tell me more". They will make time to be present with broken hearts instead of closing off all chances of communicating feelings.

Walls or bridges? Learn to recognize them. They are what they are for a reason. Just accept them and find the person who allows the healthy conversation to happen.

Make a list of those people in your life who have built a bridge for you to share emotions. Also, cherish their contact information and realize you can reach out to them at any time.

ARE YOU CONTAGIOUS?

Are you contagious? That is always a good question to ask, especially in our pandemic unstable society…but I am not referring to being contagious physically.

Oxford Languages reveals 2 definitions of the word "contagious":

1. *Spread of a disease from one person or organism to another by direct or indirect contact.*
2. *An emotion, feeling, or attitude likely to spread to and affect others.*

We can be contagious emotionally. Our attitudes can spread and impact those around us. Imagine that.

I have put this to the test…and it is true. Often when I meet someone with a big frown on their face, I try to make eye contact, smile and greet them. Immediately they smile in return and speak to me. Smiles are contagious. If you do not believe me, try giving your smile to someone who needs one…and watch them light up.

Acts of kindness are contagious. Random acts of kindness need to be more than just a motto. Let's commit to giving 1 random act of kindness early in the day and watch how it spreads to others.

Did your loved one have a particular personality or character trait that was contagious? What part of them rubbed off onto other people? You might even consider making it part of your character, a way to honor their life and memory.

COMFORT ZONES

You need to "pick your battles!" I have heard those words for years and believe them to mean we should choose which life situations require us to confront others or issues that are contrary to our beliefs.

Picking battles is pretty good advice for marriage. There will be some issues that are just not worth the time, effort, and emotions involved to confront. But, there will be other times that issues are part of building the relationship and understanding each other on a deeper emotional level.

Life as a griever is similar. Some well-meaning people will say some very insensitive and hurtful things. Our response can range from ignoring them to taking time to "educate them" on the impact their words and actions can have.

Every griever responds differently. Find your normal and comfortable place for responding. Circumstances, locations, personalities, and timing can all be factors in the decision to "pick your battles".

"Sometimes all you can do is smile. Move on with your day, hold back the tears and pretend you are OK". (coriano.com)

My personality is low key, avoiding confrontations when possible. My childhood role models did not have confrontations in front of the kids. I suspect they were all kept behind closed doors. LOL

So yes, I have learned to "pick my battles" and walk away from those that would emotionally drain me without having any clear-cut agreement.

Find your level, seek your comfort zone that will best help you emotionally, physically, and spiritually.

THE ABSOLUTE MAYBE

Years ago I wrote a silly little love song. The concept relates to how a girl might give a "non-committal" answer to her boyfriend's marriage proposal.

Today I realized we are entering what can be a very uncomfortable time of year for many on the grief journey. During the holidays there will be invitations to family parties, friends get together, work parties, and church functions. These invitations can look harmless, but for someone who is dealing with the absence of their loved one…attending can be a very difficult and emotional time.

It is time to care for yourself, you have the right to say "NO", you can decline any invitation. Protect your time because your heart is still fragile and sensitive.

Perhaps the chorus of my love song can give some good "non-committal" language to respond to the invitations.

"It's an absolute maybe, a definite could be,

Don't jump to conclusions what the answer might be.

I will think it over, it's easy you see.

It's an absolute maybe, a definite could be."

54

Actually, grievers do not owe anyone an explanation for declining an invitation. You can decline, thank them for the invitation, but at this time it is best for you to decline. You do not have to give a reason, it is self-care...and you deserve it.

TURNING DOWN INVITATIONS

Invitations to some events may be emotionally difficult. These can happen throughout the year, but especially during the holidays. Here are some ideas I heard recently.

* When you accept the invitation, inform the host that you may leave early, and for them to not take it personally.

* Drive yourself so you are not trapped in a location where you are uncomfortable. There can be emotional freedom knowing you can drive away if necessary.

* Meet someone outside the event and walk in together. Part of the anxiety can be walking into an event alone.

* Identify a place, or a room, where you can escape for a short time. Perhaps taking a short walk for a breath of fresh air will provide the needed break.

* Ahead of time, arrange for an "emotional bouncer". This person will be with you the entire time of the event. They can divert uncomfortable subjects or conversations, and might even lead you to a safer location.

Finally, just be practical by guarding your physical and emotional energy.

DEPRESSION AND FEELING ALONE

"I used to think that the worst thing in life was to end up all alone. It's not. The worst thing in life is ending up with people who make you feel alone" -Robin Williams

Robin Williams was a popular American actor and comedian. He was known for his keen ability to create characters on the spur of a moment. Unfortunately, Robin Williams died by suicide on August 11, 2014. It is possible to be surrounded by family and friends, and still feel alone. We can feel alone in a crowd.

There will be times when anyone can feel alone and depressed. No one is exempt. What can we do if we feel overwhelmed?

- Get professional help, reach out for support. It is OK
- Find like minded people, look for common interests with others
- Get active. Exercise, join a gym or an exercise group
- Chat online, try chat groups that discuss subjects you are interested in. Be open to learn new skills
- Write your thoughts and feelings in a journal. Spend time to read what you have written months ago to detect progress being made.

- Volunteer to assist with a non-profit
  organization meeting the needs of others

Do not give up. Fight and resist any urge to become isolated. Just by reading this, you are connected with others who care about your life situation. Trust others to help discover options for support. You are worth it.

WHAT IF?

Growing up, I was told to "listen to your parents". Then it was "listen to your teachers". Later it was "listen to your spouse". Then, "listen to your children".

As I have aged, and hopefully matured in some areas, I hear "listen to your doctors". But, there is one area that seems to be the most important, and often overlooked..."Listen to your body". We begin a relationship with our body from our moment of birth, and yet the zeal for life can push aside warning messages from our own body.

As I'm writing this article, I am #24 in a line of cars, waiting to be tested for COVID. My body made me aware of some changes going on. So, out of caution, I want to rule out the rampant virus in our nation.

It is quite common for grievers to replay situations with their loved one who died. There can be the "What if we had acted quicker?", "What if we had the tests run sooner?", "What if...?", "What if...?".

We can do nothing about the "What if?" statements now. The best response is to learn from them, and make intentional efforts to avoid them in the future. Yes, early detection, regular check-ups, and listening to the signals our body gives to us are all very important.

Grief has an emotional component we are all aware of. But grief also has a physical component that can often be controlled under the care of a physician who understands and is sensitive to anxiety and depression. Let's listen to our body signals. It is wise to invest into our own well- being and health.

THE REPURPOSED LIFE

Since 1983, the word "repurposed" has become popular in the English language. It basically means "to adapt for a new purpose". We see it often in furniture and accessories, re-creating a new purpose for a familiar item.

NOTE: Some readers are ready to accept the content of this article, and some are not ready. That is OK either way. It is written for those who see the application in their life, with no room for judgment.

How do we adapt in grief? How do we find purpose now? How do we 'repurpose" life now?

- Accept the reality of the loss. It really did happen
- Actively seek ways to honor the life and memory of your loved one
- Blend grief into your lifestyle, there will be good moments and bad moments each day
- Allow all emotions, from tears to laughter
- Make sure your loved one is never forgotten
- Keep their name alive and active, say their name, display photos
- Identify their heart, their passion, their purpose, and develop ways to keep it active
- To repurpose is a process, it takes time, it takes patience

A STOP DOING LIST

They come in all shapes and sizes, they are often created daily by some folks, others just make them at the beginning of a New Year.

What are they? "To Do Lists"! Perhaps you are in the habit of writing down things you want to accomplish, then mark them off your list when they are completed. I like that, in fact, it is a method I use almost daily.

But I saw something recently that caught my attention. It was a notepad, the page was full of lines, and across the top in large letters were the words "STOP DOING LIST". Can you imagine writing down things we need to STOP doing instead of things we need to do? This can be interesting. How can this relate to the grief journey?

- STOP isolating ourselves. Reach out to family and friends by telephone or social media. Look for safe outlets to meet new people with common interests, expand your friend list.
- STOP avoiding the name of your loved one who died. In fact, intentionally use their name and share memories of them. How others react and respond is not your business. However, it is your business to have a healthy grief journey.

- STOP finding excuses why you can't live out your dreams. It IS possible to set personal goals for health, for activities, and for a career. These goals will look different for everyone, but they all require a "get-r-done" attitude.
- STOP hanging around negative people. People we surround ourselves with will either build us up or tear us down. They will be givers or they will be takers. We do not have the extra energy to be drained by other people.

What will you have on your "STOP DOING LIST"?

FIND YOUR HAPPY PLACE

"Alone time is when I distance myself from the voices of the world so I can hear my own" -Maya Angelou

How do you do it? What intentional ways do you pull away from the voices of the world so you can hear your own thoughts? If you have not developed this way to implement self-care, let me encourage you to seek the method that works best for you.

For over 25 years, I have found working in clay gives me that escape from the world. When I am sculpting, I am in my "own little world" of creativity. Recently, a new hobby of coin collecting provides the same sense of self care and putting an invisible wall between me and the world around me.

Think about it. Our minds, our attitudes, and our actions can be impacted by our surroundings and the voices of others. We need to develop a way to distance ourselves from TV and news reports, from social media, from family and friends, from the pressures at work, and from stressful situations we cannot change.

Find your unique place and method to put an invisible wall between your thoughts and the constant voices of others seeking to dominate your time and thoughts. It may take practice. It may take trial and errors to discover your "happy place".

DECISIONS, DECISIONS, DECISIONS

Decisions…decisions…decisions! Often, we can get overwhelmed with the decisions that must be made, especially if there is a time deadline to them. Some people have learned to procrastinate, putting off making decisions, and letting things work themselves out. That method does not always work well, and it is not always the wise thing to do.

So, how can we make decisions with a mind that is impacted with the emotions of grief, and combined with a reduced energy level? This can be difficult, so do not be surprised to know that many face these issues. You are not alone.

First, deal with the big decisions right away. Decisions that impact lifestyles and living arrangements need to be addressed because many other decisions are based upon their outcomes. If needed, involve a trusted friend, or another family member, in making these decisions. It helps to talk through the choices and look at options. Often someone with a different viewpoint can be a good guide and see options that may be overlooked.

Write down options to the decisions that need to be made. Explore how each option would look, and what the end result might be. Then choose the option that looks and sounds best to you.

It is best to not rush through decisions if time will allow. Remember, the thought process during grief can be slowed and foggy, so time can help the understanding of choices to be made. Follow this procedure with each decision that needs to be made. Go your speed, do not rush.

BROKEN CRAYONS

"We are all a little broken. But last time I checked, broken crayons still color the same" -Trent Shelton

I believe this quote gives a visual we can relate to. Perhaps we experienced opening a new box of crayons as a child. There was always excitement, and it seemed the crayon boxes got bigger each year with the addition of the latest color fad.

We would use these crayons until there was only a very short piece to hold onto...but it still colored the same. I can even recall friends breaking a crayon in half so they could both have that special color. Broken crayons DID still color the same.

As adults, we can relate to having a broken heart. Deaths of family and friends will create a sadness and heartache that does not seem to go away. Our routines change, our life changes, priorities change, the future changes...change is constant.

Just as broken crayons can still be used to add color...we can still be useful with a broken heart. Of course, we are never the same, but our challenge will be to make a difference in lives each day. We can discover ways to "add some color" to another person as they are dealing with a heavy burden.

BACK TALKERS

"Don't worry about those who talk behind your back, they are behind you for a reason" (curiano.com)

There is a statement I adopted early in my grief support work: Grief will bring the best out of some people, and it will bring the worst out of others. Haven't you noticed it to be the truth? After a loss, some people will be very sincere, helpful, and respectful to others. We need these people, their support and presence can be a life saver. We know these people will be there for us, they will not judge us, they will be a good friend, and a constant strength to draw from.

We are also aware of those who seem to become toxic to a griever. These people may say inappropriate things, their words and actions may seem to disregard the grief of those around them. There may be a tendency to make the grief "about them" instead of forming a strong bond with others who are hurting.

Yes, we are aware there will be those who talk behind our back at a time of loss. Some want to know all the facts so they can be a source of information, others will continue to share rumors or inappropriate comments.

THE BUSY BODY

"Busy-body: A meddling or prying person" (Oxford Language Dictionary)

This type of person is often referred to as a "gossip" also. They cannot help offering advice to friends, whether they want it or not. Do you know this type of nosy person? Their usual activity is to pry into areas that are none of their business. They like to be the first with the facts, and often they make up what they do not know. It is their style.

As you read these words, someone probably came to mind that meets the description. Their actions can be very hurtful and frustrating, especially during a time of loss and grief. Here are some suggestions on how to cope with the busy-bodies around us:

- Remain vague with answers
- Choose to limit the information you share
- Set boundaries that make you comfortable
- Learn these statements and repeat as needed:
    o "I'd prefer not to talk about that"
    o "That's a little too personal"
    o "I'm sorry, but that is private information"
    o "I'd rather not say"
- And to really get the point across, begin each of these statements with the strong word of "NO!".

Take control of the conversation with busy-bodies. You cannot hurt their feelings. They do not have feelings, or they would not be doing the damage they do.

YOUR BODYGUARD

Have you ever had a bodyguard? Think about it.

A bodyguard can provide you with security and protection when you need it the most and give you peace of mind. It can be very helpful to have a bodyguard in life...not the type that can be hired...but the one who does it out of love and devotion.

Physical bodyguards can provide a sense of greater safety, security, and protection when they are around.

Emotional bodyguards have the ability to provide comfort and support during times of stress and high anxiety...they can provide assurance and peace of mind.

Spiritual bodyguards can serve as a trusted guide in matters of the heart and soul. They can be a faith leader to provide Spiritual centering and calmness.

Already you many think of those who have been a "bodyguard" to you in many ways. These are important relationships to be appreciated and nurtured. Unfortunately, death can remove a bodyguard in a moment. The feelings of being secure and protected can be replaced with fears, anxieties, and being vulnerable.

71

This can impact sleeping, eating, and concentration. Seeking professional help and advice during these times can be beneficial. Professional help is not a sign of weakness…rather, it is a sign of strength and taking control over your own mental health. It is worth the risk…don't you think?

BEING ON TIME, OR EARLY

"Better three hours too soon than a minute too late" -*William Shakespeare*

Some people are known by family and friends for always being late…always, it never fails.

A punctual person is all about respecting the time of others, it takes discipline and dedication. Being punctual helps build strong character; and can lead to being more successful in life.

By now you know where YOU fit into this description. Perhaps we can all work to improve in the area of being punctual and respectful for the time schedule of others.

How did your loved one do in this area? Were they always ahead of time…right on time…or always late? We just learn to adjust to the schedules of those we love.

Many successful business leaders believe that if you are "on time" for a monthly meeting you are late for that meeting. The statement is often made that "if it is important, it is important to arrive early".

Punctuality can be a challenge for grievers. It will take intentional decisions and increased commitment to be punctual for all meetings. It is a great discipline to begin with.

MAKE A LIST

It was something I was taught at an early age, and it becomes more valuable as I get older. In a speech class, I was taught to make "bullet points" of any speech. Then, if the speech gets off track and off subject, the outline guides me to the subject again.

Basically, it is a way to stay organized. Speaking to a group can create some anxiety, so an outline can help focus on the message needing to be expressed. There will be many potential distractions, but a plan can help stay on purpose.

Life can be like this. Our good intentions can be thrown off by the smallest distractions. We may even feel defeated because we did not achieve what we intended. But, there can be remedy, a help.

Try this: begin each day by writing down a list of "things to do today". Not in great detail, just a list of things you would like to accomplish by the end of the day. About halfway through the day, look at the list. Mark off those things that were completed, and make plans to complete the next one on the list.

This process helps with focus and concentration. It is very easy to enter a mental fog and not see a focus or purpose. This list will remind you of necessary items that need to be completed.

THE BODY CLOCK

Britannica dictionary defines "body clock" as a system in the body that controls when you need to sleep, eat, etc. Once a body clock system is disturbed, it takes time for it to get adjusted to a normal and comfortable pattern again.

Has your "body clock" ever been off of it's normal pattern? It can really mess up a sleep schedule. It is possible to reset a sleeping pattern, but it may take time.

- Do not nap, even if you feel tired. Instead of napping, try taking a walk or exercising
- Get up at the same time each morning. Do not sleep in, even if you feel tired…force yourself to get out of bed. I know a lady who makes her bed the first thing each morning so she is not tempted to get back into it. Perhaps that will be a helpful routine for you
- Avoid exercising too close to bedtime, it may prevent your body from relaxing
- Watch what you eat close to bedtime. Try to avoid snacks with sugar, caffeine, and nicotine…..all are stimulants
- Take a warm bath, listen to relaxing music, or do something else you find relaxing. Some people find reading helps calm the mind and body before bedtime

After a loss, it is normal for sleeping and eating patterns to be disrupted. Our body clock is upset, so it takes an intentional effort to create an atmosphere to sleep. If this becomes a real health issue, consult with your physician for a sleep aid. But remember, relief from grief does not come in pill form.

PRACTICE, PRACTICE, PRACTICE

I was watching a physical therapist working with our daughter since her recent stroke. It dawned on me that we need to focus on what we CAN control. If we spend too much time thinking about what we cannot control or change, we could magnify the feelings of hopelessness.

Giving attention to the things we CAN control will help us feel more capable. It can provide a greater sense of urgency and give us the motivation and energy to work toward making progress.

We must practice acceptance. Acknowledging the things outside of our control may actually improve our ability to accept them. Feeling like we have to control everything can actually lead to being overwhelmed by the reality of the situation.

Most people like to be in control at all times. But when we are dealing with the loss of a loved one, it may seem every area of life has changed and out of control. Here are some steps that have helped others to deal with change and challenges:

- Acknowledge the changes you are experiencing, do not try to deny them
- Consider solutions to the challenges being faced

- Plan for a time for yourself...a mental health break for a change of scenery
- Remember things you enjoy in life, plan ahead to enjoy them again
- Talk to a trusted friend about your feelings
- Look for one area you CAN control...and focus on it.

PRACTICE MAKES PROGRESS

I have always heard "practice makes perfect". Well, I have practiced a lot of things in my lifetime…baseball, basketball, fishing, sculpting, and several more hobbies and interests. I have never reached the point of perfection in any of them. I only realized I needed more practice in all of them.

Recently, I read a quote I will adopt instead of "practice makes perfect".

Mark Hawthorne (QUOTESSTATS.COM) says "practice makes progress".

I can relate to that, and it does not seem to put extra stress on trying to achieve something out of reach.

This can relate to the grief journey…and perhaps it can lower the levels of anxiety and stress we place upon ourselves with personal expectations. After a loss, it can be very stressful and emotional to join friends for social gatherings. "Practice makes progress". Follow through with the commitment, accept the invitation…but, always have a plan of escape if things get too uncomfortable or emotional.

It is OK to step away, it is OK to retreat to your safe place without needing to make any excuses. It is called self-care, to be allowed, accepted, and admired. "Practice makes progress".

If the social adventure does not feel comfortable, get to your comfort zone. But, realize "practice makes progress". At some point, when you are ready, accept another invitation to step out of your emotional/grief comfort zone.

KEEP MOVING

As I merged into traffic on a turnpike, I saw those words on a sign, bright and bold. Evidently, there is a problem with drivers stopping at the merge point of traffic...not a smart thing to do.

I chuckled at the simple message of "KEEP MOVING". Those were the exact words my cardiologist and my family doctor had instructed me to do..."KEEP MOVING". Diet and exercise seems to be their constant repetition to everyone, and "KEEP MOVING". The idea is to stay active, don't give up, don't quit, don't sit still.

Grievers need to hear these words also..."KEEP MOVING". It would be very easy to give into the impulse of pulling into a ball, covering up the head, and staying in bed. Many want to do that, but they have kids to care for, pets to tend to, or jobs that require them to be there and draw a paycheck.

But pulling into a shell does not make the pain go away. We take the pain into the shell with us and that can produce guilt, regrets, and lead down the slippery slope into depression.

So, the best advice is like I've received from the medical community...."KEEP MOVING"!

CHECK THE FILTERS

Every car has 4 main filter systems: air filter, oil filter, fuel filter, and cabin filter. These filters enable free flows and catch contaminants in the air, impurities in the fuel, and dust in the oil. We are always advised to "check the filters" to prevent problems.

Often a disease process can bring on a sudden change in personality. It is not that people are intentionally rude and say hurtful things...but perhaps their "filter" needs to be checked. A chemical imbalance in the blood can cause sudden and drastic changes in health and personality.

The stress of grief can also impact the entire system. Grief can lower the immune system, causing emotional outbursts. The thought process can change, and memory can be impacted as well. The most simple decisions can feel monumental when the stress of grief is heavy.

When energy levels remain low, if sleeping and eating patterns are not consistent...it may be time for a visit to a physician. Simple blood tests can reveal a chemical imbalance in the blood or other bodily functions that need attention. It is not a sign of weakness to seek the opinion of a physician. Actually, it is a sign of wisdom and caring for ourselves.

HINDSIGHT OR KINDSIGHT?

"Hindsight is always twenty twenty" -Billy Wilder

Isn't that the truth? We can all look back at decisions in life and consider choices that might have been better. The process of looking back can create some uncertainty or doubt…a look at what could have been different.

Recently I saw a twist in this quote: "View your life with KINDSIGHT. Stop beating yourself up about things from your past. Instead of slapping your forehead and asking "What was I thinking?" breathe and ask the kinder question "What was I learning?" (Kate Donnelly)

Life-long lessons can come from a difficult time. Perhaps we can see how things could have been avoided altogether…but that is "hindsight"…looking back. As the quote says, "Instead of slapping our forehead and asking "what was I thinking?" breathe and ask the KINDER question :"What was I learning?"

Can you do that yet? It is OK if you can't look back and see something you learned. Everyone is different, some people recognize the life lessons quickly…others take longer. That does not make It bad…only different.

But we do learn from life. We learn from the painful events. We must apply "KINDSIGHT" to our hindsight. The first person we should be KINDER to is ourself.

OPINIONS

I have noticed lately that I have very little patience with people who share "their opinion" of things…especially when their opinion is not requested! I realize everyone has an opinion on everything, it is only natural. But when we are confronted by someone who begins to express their "personal opinion" when it is not asked for…it can present a challenge.

It reminds me of the old saying: "There are 2 ways to do something…my way and the wrong way". Usually, I find those who share their opinions without being asked for it are offended if we do not immediately adopt their opinions as our own.

People will have an opinion as how long a person should grieve. They will share their opinion on the steps that must be taken to "get on with your life". Some will even express when to go back to work, or when to sell the house, or when to start social gatherings again.

I've learned some key words that raise a flag of concern for me. When someone begins a statement with "Well, this is what you NEED to do…you NEED to…".

In grief, one size does not fit all. One approach does not work in all counseling. One style of dealing with loss does not work for everyone. Every loss is unique for each individual...thus, coping with loss will be different for each person.

We need to identify those who blindly spout their opinions, and realize "their opinion" and "their method" does not necessarily need to become ours. (In my opinion)

END OF THE ROPE

"When you're at the end of your rope, tie a knot and hold on" (Theodore Roosevelt)

I have heard this quote for many years, but never really thought of how it could be applied to life. After a loss, there can be many times it feels we are at the "end of our rope". That implies an end, nowhere else to turn, and out of options. To "tie a knot" means we are making definite decisions and taking actions to keep from falling.

But, how do we "tie a knot and hold on" at those times? Tying a knot means creating a better grip, getting a better hold, gaining some confidence that we will not fall. Let's consider what this could look like for someone in grief:

- Return to the basics in life: simplify each day, change routines to make things easier
- Take 1 step at a time: progress is made moving forward steadily at a comfortable speed for you
- Focus on tasks: concentrate on the details to complete 1 task, only 1, only 1 at a time
- Express feelings: the opposite is to hold the feelings inside, creating internal problems and long term damage

- Self-care: take a deep breath that is NOT a sigh. Make intentional changes in nutrition, sleep, and exercise patterns
- Write your life story/love story: blend photos and stories. Give the end result to family members as a gift
- In reality, we are all just "holding on"…so, let's practice more patience and kindness

LIMP HOME MODE

I have heard the ideal term! Our car was having problems accelerating, then suddenly would not go faster than 10 miles per hour. I researched the problem and discovered it was a sensor related to the accelerator pedal. In order to prevent the pedal from sticking at a fast speed, it automatically enters a mode called the "limp home mode". It is OK to drive at a slow speed, short distances to get home while arranging for repairs. "Limp Home Mode" describes it well.

I think grief has that mode also. Things change after a death, everything changes. Our forward progress changes, the speed which we do things will change, our attitude can change…everything changes. We enter our own "limp home mode".

After a loss, our productivity and initiative may take a severe setback. Instead of leading the pack, we may feel like we are simply in the "limp home mode" each day.

This can become obvious with our energy level and motivation following a loss. Getting out of bed may drain our physical and our emotional energy. Our motivation may be gone completely, and it can be very difficult to push ourselves to accomplish even the smallest of tasks. Yes, the "limp home mode" can enter the grief journey.

So, what can be done? For a car, it is turned over to the experts who know the inner workings of an automobile. They have "tools" to detect the problem and solve it. Seeking professional help is not a sign of weakness, it is a sign of wisdom. Hoping things will change does not fix a problem. Trusting those who are specialists can be a very wise choice to address and overcome the "limp home mode".

ADDING LIFE TO YEARS

"And in the end, it is not the years in your life that count. It's the life in your years." (Abraham Lincoln)

Act your age! That is a pretty straight forward comment. It is usually addressed to someone involved in behavior that is not approved for someone of their years.

If you did not know your actual age in years and months, how old do you feel? We have all met people whose appearance and attitude were much older than their actual age. Then we have also met people who are full of the energy and enthusiasm of someone much younger than their actual age.

Little babies and children have influenced my life and taught me as many life lessons as older adults. The number of their years did not matter. They possessed insight into life far beyond their years.

Also, I have known some who had a long life but seemed to be unhappy and miserable as they aged. It seems to be a pattern that these folks desire to make those around them miserable also. It is best to avoid spending a lot of time around these folks if possible.

Look for ways to add life to your years. Dream, make plans to learn new things, meet new people, travel as possible, experience new things. If physical travel is limited, take advantage of libraries, books, classes, and online offerings.

Let's push excuses aside and add life to our years. It will benefit us and also those around us.

POTENTIAL

Years ago, I listened to the radio interview of a professional basketball star. During the interview, the host mentioned a rising young player with "potential". The wise and experienced player made a profound statement. He said "potential just means it has not happened yet". Just having potential does not mean success or championships.

This can also apply to grief. There can be a lot of areas with "potential". There is "potential" of getting a restful nights sleep...it has not happened yet.

There is "potential" of going through an entire day without being overcome with emotions related to a loved one...it has not happened yet.

There can be "potential" of hearing a song that brings back memories without melting into a pool of tears...it has not happened yet.

There can be "potential" of meeting someone and risking being emotionally vulnerable...but it has not happened yet.

There is "potential" of moving from a familiar home and starting over...but it has not happened yet.

There can be a lot of "potential" in the grief journey....things that have not happened yet. It is OK...it is OK...it is OK.

Do not attempt to move ahead until you are ready physically, emotionally, and spiritually. It is your journey, your pace, your grief.

There will be a time you can look back and see the progress you have made. Congratulate yourself on the small steps you complete. "Potential" is reached one step at a time.

MOURNING NOTES:

<u>MOURNING NOTES:</u>

MEMORY CONNECTIONS

THE JUNK DRAWER

We were visiting in the home of friends recently, and I had a "flashback" memory of my dad. It was unexpected, no warning, and seemed to be so minor that no one else noticed. But, to me it brought back some very special memories of my dad.

The friend was looking for something in the kitchen, and she made the statement, "I will look in the junk drawer". Everyone knew what she was talking about. I grew up in a home that had a "junk drawer". We have one in our home, always have, and always will. My dad always added to the "junk drawer".

The "junk drawer" is the storage place for all the extra pieces, the leftover items, the rare and unique items. It is the place to put things we might need someday. One thing is certain and is a proven fact. We will never need anything from the "junk drawer" UNTIL we have thrown it away…then we will need something from that drawer.

A "junk drawer" may seem to be such a silly and insignificant reminder of a loved one who has died. But, to me it is a very valuable link to memories. The "junk drawer" was important to my dad, it connects our memories.

Is there something similar, something others might feel is "insignificant", that connects your memory to someone? It may be certain foods, a song, a car, a location, a movie, a certain clothing style. Everyone is unique in their journey through grief. It really helps to recognize those areas that may cause a "flashback" of memories. They may cause us to laugh, smile, or even shed healthy tears.

SENSE THEIR PRESENCE

A few nights ago my wife picked up our young great-grandson. She hugged him tightly, then said "he smells just like a baby...I love that smell"! Of course, it might have been the smell of baby lotion, or perhaps baby powder. Regardless of the source, she caught the scent of what we know as a "baby smell". There is nothing like it.

Adults can carry a particular scent also. It may be a favorite perfume, a regular after shave, or even the unique scent of the skin. But we can have a certain scent that others identify as "our scent".

After a death, these scents can become even more special. We may intentionally keep their scent around to provide needed support and memories. Perhaps we even spray their scent on our clothing to "sense their presence".

Do not be ashamed or embarrassed by capturing these fragrances. Seek them out, intentionally blend their scent into your own lifestyle. No excuses needed...go for it.

Remember, we lose people physically, but emotionally we never lose them. Scents are a way to mix memories with a fragrance or smell. Allow them to bring laughter, smiles, and even tears.

TREASURES WE KEEP

"This belonged to my grandmother"

"This has been passed down through our family for generations"

"My grandfather carried this, so it is important for me to keep it"

Are you familiar with similar statements regarding physical objects that have been kept, treasured, and passed down through families? These objects can be very special and should be kept in a safe place to continue passing them down through the family line.

But, somewhere, sometime, someone had to decide "what to keep and what to get rid of" after a death. The choices ranged from keeping everything in boxes that collect dust, to displaying a few of these treasures, to discarding everything and have nothing that connects to those who are gone. There will be individual preferences, big decisions, and the realization that not everyone shares the same opinion on this process of keeping or discarding. Not everyone will agree on the importance of these treasures.

A gentleman's wife died, the ladies in the church thought they would help him adjust to life without her. They took every item of clothing and jewelry that belonged to his wife and made a big donation to the local second-hand store. Guess where this gentleman was the very next morning….at the second-hand store looking for "memories". Often an object may seem simple and insignificant to others, but it can be very meaningful to someone with a broken heart searching for memories.

  The best approach is to make these decisions gradually and get input from others, family members and friends, consider the options. Each situation is different and needs to be respected.

PLANTING FLOWERS IN LIFE

"If I could plant a flower for every time I miss you, I could walk through my garden forever" (unknown)

Missing a loved one who has died can be the deepest and most constant pain a person will suffer in a lifetime. Once a lady described her grief pain to me as "a deep longing to be with someone you love more than life itself".

The descriptive word that was most prevalent to me after my father died was the feeling of being "homesick". He is home, and I am not. You will discover words to use that will best describe your grief pain. That feeling word may change over time.

The quote above brings out the obvious for a griever...we MISS them. Missing someone is not just for a few hours, days, or even for a few years. We will miss them for the remainder of our life because there is a big hole where they lived in our presence.

Expect to miss someone...you are not alone. Every person we meet during the day is missing someone. Some are open to talk about the person they miss, others keep silent and allow the grief to gnaw upon the peace that seems to disappear.

It is a beautiful thought, planting a flower every time we miss someone. Indeed, we would be surrounded by flowers each step of our days. We will walk through this garden of flowers (memories) for the rest of our days. Take time to notice and smell the flowers around you.

Perhaps our action of planting a flower when we miss them is to speak to a stranger, do a kind deed, or seek some way to mention their name to someone. Planting flowers of a memory makes the journey a little prettier...perhaps.

DID YOU SMELL THAT?

Do you realize we each carry around our own unique scent? A fragrance on our skin or our clothing? In fact, it is quite possible others identify us with a certain smell. Amazing, isn't it?

My grandparents on my dad's side leave me with the memory of smelling snuff in their home and on their clothing. Both dipped snuff, had a spit can on the floor, and the snuff smell burned the nostrils.

My mom's mother had a fragrance of bath powder on her skin…always. Hugging her left the image of a fragrant powder puff, applied in ample supply.

Even when my dad's clothing was clean it still carried a scent from his work as a mechanic. The combo of sweat and grease is not soon forgotten.

Have you intentionally captured the scent of a loved one? I encourage you to purchase a fragrance that connects to memories of them. Perhaps releasing the fragrance around the house is comforting, or it may be something for personal reflections as you spray it on clothing or in a closet.

Do not be ashamed or embarrassed by connecting to a fragrance. God provided our senses to be used, and they can become connections to memories of loved ones. It is OK to cry and smile…while sensing their unique fragrance and presence. It is OK!

HEARTPRINTS

"Be the things you loved about the people who are gone"

It is a phrase I use many times in my writings and speaking opportunities. We need to "honor our loved ones". By honoring their memory, we are declaring that they lived, and their life served a very special purpose in this world.

Their fingerprints are left behind on physical items. But their "heartprint" is also pressed deeply into the lives of family members and friends. These imprints are forever, never to be forgotten.

Their life can be honored with memorial services, tributes, the naming of fundraisers, scholarships, and hundreds of other worthwhile efforts. But there is a way to honor someone that is often overlooked, and anyone can do it. This effort does not cost anything, but it pays priceless dividends to the heart.

The secret? BE the things you LOVED MOST about them. Imitate their passion in life, care as they cared, love as they loved.

Let your life be an extension of their heart. THAT is the way to honor a loved one.

TAKING A MEMORY PICTURE

I just read a term that challenged me. In an article about noticing the beauty around us, and those special moments we often overlook, I read the term "take a memory picture". I like that.

When I see something that is beautiful and touches my heart in a special way...I am going to "take a memory picture" of it. I will intentionally close my eyes for a moment, envision the image, and then open my eyes. The intent is to "take a memory picture".

Even if I cannot recall the image later, that is OK. I was able to capture and enjoy the moment in a "memory picture" at the time.

Can you imagine doing this with your special loved one? Or while looking at beautiful scenery? Take a "memory picture" in that place you never want to forget.

Photos are great, but if we can pull images into our mind instantly because we "took a memory picture" of the moment...that is a treasure.

Let's seek to "take a memory picture" today. You will know the moment, you will know the time. Use your eyes as the camera, and your intentional blink as the shutter to capture the moment.

REPUTATIONS

Reputation: "the beliefs or opinions that are generally held about someone or something. An understood belief that someone or something has a particular habit or characteristic".

Most of us get reputations in life, some are intentionally earned, others just happen and we carry labels throughout our lifetime. Did your loved one have a good reputation? A good reputation could be that they were known to be honest, kind, and a hard worker. But how do we build a reputation? Here are some ideas:

- Keep your promises so people believe your word
- Have a positive personality with a habit of encouraging others
- Give more than expected in every situation, go beyond the call of duty
- Be open to help others

Was your loved one known for their honesty? Did others notice their unique sense of humor? Did they go out of their way to help others? Did people ask for their opinion because of their wisdom? Were they known as a loyal person? What was their reputation?

Do you realize we honor the reputation of our loved one when we compliment others? When we acknowledge positive attributes in someone, we are

Bob Willis
MOURNING MOMENTS

helping form their reputation. As we help build the reputation of others, we are actually working on our own reputation. Interesting how that works. I've always heard that "what goes around comes around".

109

EASY HELLO, PAINFUL GOODBYE

"You were my easiest HELLO, and my most painful GOODBYE"

Recently I saw this saying on a sign in an antique store. It spoke volumes to me. It puts into words what I see over and over again in posts from grievers. A very true and powerful statement. In fact, when many of you read this statement...you envisioned the face of a loved one.

Some people are easy to meet, a very comfortable feeling from the start. These people are not threatening, they are usually kind, considerate of others, and exude a positive attitude that is contagious. In our lifetime we will meet many people, but perhaps someone was the "easiest HELLO".

It seems the "easiest HELLO" relationships can often lead to becoming soul mates. There is a connection on a different level...on the heart and soul level. It may even feel like you have known them for a much longer time.

Just as some "HELLO" moments are different, the "GOODBYE" moments can be very different also. We have all experienced deaths of friends, and family members, and they all hurt. The loss of anyone close to us can bring sadness because it ends the physical relationship.

But, the "most painful GOODBYE" changes our life. We are never the same because it seems we had to say goodbye to part of our own heart. For some, the "most painful GOODBYE" was the death of a child, others can identify with this feeling because a spouse died, and still others feel this pain due to the death of a parent or other close family member.

A painful loss can be any relationship that was very special, closer than others, and a heart connection. Our losses should never be compared with the losses of other people, but our heart will tell us the name of our "most painful GOODBYE". I am sorry you can relate to this pain, and I pray you find comfort from others who have experienced this grief. You are not alone.

CEMETERY THERAPY

Last week I was early for an appointment, so I took time in a nearby cemetery for some "cemetery therapy". I know it sounds morbid to some, but I enjoy walking through old cemeteries, reading the headstone information of people I never got to meet. Etched into those granite and marble markers are words meant to last forever. Most inscriptions will mention family, faith, service to our Country, or references to Heaven.

Then I saw it! I had to read the name several times, I looked closely at the dates on the marker. It was her! This marker was placed to mark the burial site for a friend's wife. It made me aware of some things:

- Seeing a person's name on a headstone can immediately produce a visual image of them in the mind. For me at least, these images always capture this person laughing, smiling, and enjoying life.

- It is important to have a "place" to go to, a "place" that shouts of their memory, their life and the need for them to be remembered. This may be in a cemetery, or a mountain top, or an ocean, or a mantle in the

home…but a "place' is important to connect
to their memory.

- A slab of plain granite has no emotions
  attached to it. But, inscribing the name of a
  loved one, confirming dates of birth and
  death, and perhaps adding words of
  memory…suddenly the cold granite slab takes
  on a new meaning and emotional power.

I remembered my friend and his wife, and I walked
away with thankfulness that our paths had
crossed. Also thankful for the brief "cemetery
therapy".

REMEMBERED OR MISSED?

Payne Stewart was an American professional golfer. He won 11 PGA tour events, including 3 major championships. Personally, I remember his smooth golf swing and his very stylish golf clothing. Payne Stewart was very popular with the fans and his fellow golfers.

Tragically, Payne Stewart died in a plane crash on October 25, 1999. His sudden death shook the golf world, and he is still remembered as a great ambassador for the game of golf.

A journalist once interviewed Payne Stewart and asked how he wanted to be remembered. He said, "I could be remembered by shots I have made, and tournaments I have played in, but those are just facts and figures. I do not want to be remembered...I want to be missed. I'm going to a special place when I die, but I want to make sure my life is special while I'm here."

It is normal to remember loved ones who died, and perhaps we can remember a great number of family and friends. But often the number of loved ones we miss can be counted on one hand. It is OK to miss someone. In fact, we miss loved ones because their life was special to us. We are challenged to live our life in such a special way, that after we die, we will not just be remembered...we will be missed.

VALUE OF PHOTOGRAPHS

Imagine a life without any photographs of loved ones. I believe it would be very sad. Under the bed at my mom's house is an Army footlocker full of photos. Most are black and white, many are school pictures of her 5 children. It is always a great time of laughter and memories when the family looks through these photographs. They are treasures.

We look at the photo of a loved one and immediately we are reminded of how they made us "feel". That is the special part…the "feeling" of a memory. They could have represented love, strength, encouragement, security, faith, and understanding. Some people even make us feel special and appreciated. Photos can remind us of those feelings, and many more.

Remember, we are also making others "feel" something by our words and actions. Our character and our personality can't be totally captured in a photo, but those around us are fully aware. We have an opportunity to make others feel needed and special. Let's do it.

AT THEIR BEST

We have all heard the terms…"they are at their best", or "They are at the top of their game". These statements can refer to someone who has exceeded expectations, gone above the call of duty, and stood out from the crowd because of their achievements.

Does this describe your loved one? How did it make you feel when you saw them "at their best"? What did it look like when that happened? What did it feel like to be around them during this time?

As we look back over relationships, we can identify areas where loved ones stood out. Can you identify the traits they had that caused them to excel in areas others did not?

As you identify these traits, I want to challenge you to honor their memory by seeking to give those traits to the world around you. Consider making a difference in lives by supporting what they loved and cared for. Perhaps it will be a big change in character for you…but it will be worth it because it is a wonderful way to honor a life.

Instead of looking back at what did NOT happen, let's look forward to what CAN happen if we focus on sharing their strong traits with others.

KILROY WAS HERE

Prehistoric cave art has always fascinated me. Over 20,000 years ago, paintings of animals and humans were made on the walls of caves scattered around the world. These crude paintings are thought to have a religious aspect, an attempt to express awareness of a belief system. Animals may have been depicted in order to summon them for a hunt that was taking place. Without a doubt, the paintings are proof that someone was saying "we were here".

"Kilroy was here". This statement was a form of graffiti from the 1940's. A bald-headed man with a big nose peeking over a wall with his hands clinging onto the wall was found in the most unusual places. U.S. servicemen would draw this character and add the statement where they were stationed or camped around the world. Again, it was a way of someone saying "we were here".

It seems we leave messages behind for family and friends to be aware that our presence will always remain. We do not need to paint symbols or figures on the walls of caves. We do not need to scribble graffiti so everyone can notice it. Our "artwork" will be on the hearts of family and friends. We leave a memory, we leave a mark, we make an impression with our life.

Each of us carry the "heart art" from a loved one who is no longer with us. They touched our life like no one else can ever do. Therefore, the memories we carry in our heart are their statement that "we were there". Let's look at this impact as a gift, a treasure, not as anything that should be avoided. They were here, and their presence will always be part of us.

A COMFORT OBJECT

It is very common in our present society to be asked to "empty your pockets/purse". New focus on security has us doing this when boarding an airplane and going through their security station. Hopefully we think ahead and not carry anything that will be confiscated or prove to be embarrassing. It is part of our present culture.

My dad always carried a pocket knife. Even when he was in the hospital recovering from a stroke, he asked for his pocket knife. Staff was hesitant to allow it, fearing he was going to harm himself or others. Family knew it was his "comfort zone", his security. We saw that he was able to hold his pocket knife, and we saw how it comforted and relaxed him.

Do you have something you carry with you? Do you have a "comfort zone" object that seems to provide some sense of security and well-being? Did your loved one have something special to them that they liked to hold on to?

Even if we cannot carry the object in public, we may have something available to us at our home. Perhaps this is connected to the "security blanket" need in many of us. These items can help reduce anxiety, they can provide emotional support during a time of stress , and can even give assurance that everything will be OK.

FIRST IMPRESSIONS

"You never get a second chance to make a first impression" -
Andrew Grant

Studies have shown that a person forms their first impression of another individual somewhere between seven seconds and two minutes.

Body language, eye contact, tone of voice, and the ability to listen to others all make you a great communicator. A warm smile and the ability to give sincere compliments go a long way with making an impression.

These are some common words to describe a positive first impression: attractive, calm, confident, friendly, genuine, happy, honest, interesting, respectful, neat, and humble. Be aware of your first impression when you meet someone.

What words would you use to describe your first impression of your loved one? After a loss, it is good to reflect upon the initial impression we had when we met them. Did your first impression prove to be accurate? Were you totally right? Or totally wrong?

Be aware, we each make first impressions with every first encounter. Remember, we only get one chance to make a first impression.

A "GPS" FOR THE GRIEF JOURNEY

This past week we took a road trip to visit relatives. The drive included travel through some cities and country that was a new route for us. So, the GPS on my phone gave excellent directions...distance, where to turn, even a change in the route to bypass stalled traffic on an interstate. All of this information helped make the trip easier and successful.

Isn't it too bad there is not a GPS for the grief journey? It would be helpful to know when memories were going to be confronted. Knowing how to make adjustments in schedules to prevent painful moments would be helpful also.

But, unfortunately, there is no GPS for the grief journey. SO, what should we expect?

- Expect simple things such as photographs or music to bring memories roaring back with mixed emotions. You may find the urge to sing along with the music, mixed with tears from a broken heart...expect it.

- Expect someone to say "magic words" that instantly remind you of your loved one and things they would have said in similar circumstances...expect it.

- Expect to hear their voice or sense their presence. This may be frightening at first, but embrace the moment. It is a reminder that we lose people physically, but emotionally and spiritually we never lose them…expect it.

- Expect to see someone who favors them; expect to smell a fragrance that they wore. Grief is emotional, emotions are attached to senses…expect it.

  Develop your own "Grief GPS" as you travel the grief journey. Learn what to expect, learn to recognize signs that emotions and memories are near. Embrace them…they are reminders of love…they are reminders of a relationship…expect it.

START COLLECTING THESE THINGS

Stuff…things…material items…we use many terms to describe the items we accumulate over time. For some it becomes a passion to collect that cannot be contained. That can lead to an abundance of "collections" and "keepsakes". Perhaps we "collect" things from the past as reminders of a life that holds many memories.

Are you a "collector" of a particular item? Was your loved one a "collector"? Was there something you both enjoyed collecting together? Collecting items can be a mutual bond and activity enjoyed together.

But priorities will change in life. Circumstances in life can change because of sickness or death. The things collected lose all of the thrill and satisfaction. In reality, we would trade every item we collected for the health and presence of someone we love. The "collections" around us can be reminders of enjoying a beautiful relationship that shared a common interest.

So, what is important to "collect" now that life has drastically changed?

- "collect" photos of a loved one
- "collect" items that hold the fingerprints of a loved one

- "collect" clothing that still carries their fragrance
- "collect" friends who let you share memories
- "collect" memories that bring smiles and tears
- "collect" life lessons to share with family and friends…write them down

THE MEMORY BOOK

"It is impossible to forget someone who gave us so much to remember" (unknown)

Read that quote again. Do you see it? It says it is IMPOSSIBLE to forget them. Put aside the fear of forgetting them, that will never happen.

Focus instead on how much they gave us to remember. Think of all the memories they left behind for us to recall.

It would be awesome to keep a "memory book" dedicated to that special person. When a memory of them crosses your mind, write it in their "memory book".

It will not take long to have a book of gifts, a special way of honoring their life and their impact upon others. It will reinforce the fact that it is impossible to forget someone who touched your life in such a special way.

Recalling how our life was touched by another person is evidence of love, respect, and a unique way to remember them. Welcome the memories, cherish that they happened.

SIGNS

The timing could not have been more perfect! I was to lead a Celebration of Life for a friend who had died. The weather was absolutely beautiful for an outdoor event. As I stepped to the front of the crowd and announced we were going to begin the program...it happened!

Between me and the seated crowd, flew the most beautiful yellow butterfly I have ever seen. It fluttered in front of the family that were seated, then flew to land on a spray of flowers at the front of the group for a few moments before fluttering away.

Everyone was amazed. You could hear the sounds of pure joy and excitement as many said, "Oh, a butterfly!". Applause and cheers broke out, as we realized this was a "special sign" for the day. Smiles were mixed with tears of joy because of the visit from a butterfly.

Not only the butterfly, but a red cardinal sat on a branch nearby and observed the events. It was truly a day of unexplained presence, comforting for family and friends. Never have I experienced anything a dramatic and meaningful to every person there.

Until I pass onto the next life, I will not understand how such things can take place. But, for now, I find comfort in the "signs" that cannot be explained.

The group that gathered for this Celebration of Life will remember these "signs" for years to come. It was an amazing experience that quickly bonded the entire group with love, comfort, and the purpose of remembering and honoring a life that was beautiful to them.

Have you observed "signs" that provided the presence of a loved one? What were they?

WARNING SIGNS

I drive a lot. Evidently my schedule and travel route is known by highway maintenance crews in surrounding states. Regardless of my route, there WILL BE road construction...no doubt.

Warning signs are visible: merge now, right lane closed ahead, left lane closed ahead, detour, reduce speed, prepare to stop, etc. Any trip must allow for unexpected road construction delays and changes.

Delays and changes can take place in the grief journey. We do not choose to travel this difficult road of grief. This road can be crowded at times with others making their way with no map, and constant obstacles.

If you could set up "warning signs" along the grief journey...what would they say? What warnings would you give to those entering this difficult journey?

At some point in life everyone will experience loss and grief. No one is exempt. There are no "experts" who have it all figured out. There are only fellow travelers who share their insight and experience with others.

From your own insight and experience, what "warning signs" should be obvious along the way?

MOURNING NOTES:

MOURNING NOTES:

EXPRESSING EMOTIONS

LOST IT OR FOUND IT?

I read a lot about the grief of individuals, a lot. Each day involves reading the gut-wrenching stories of loss and the emotions that are out of control for a long time. Everyone's loss is different. Some people are stoic and seem to be a pillar of strength for others. Then, there are those who struggle daily with the basics of getting out of bed, getting dressed, and facing the day ahead.

Often, I read where people say they are "losing it". I understand what they are saying. They mean they begin to cry, almost uncontrollable crying. It is very common to have those times of venting through tears.

But I would like to suggest a change in the wording. We have not "lost it". In fact, I think when we cry and let tears flow...we have actually "found it".

It is normal to cry after a loss. Society wants us to dry it up and get over it. We either cry on the outside or we cry on the inside. It is healthier to cry on the outside. If we cry on the inside our heart will fill up with tears and we will be aware of a heavy heart. Holding the emotions inside can cause many problems physically, emotionally, mentally, and spiritually.

So, when we cry, we have "found it", we are not "losing it". We have found the best way to express our grief emotions, no need to apologize, just tell people you have just "found it".

A HELPLESS FEELING

HELPLESS!! I have often described a helpless feeling as "trying to describe a rainbow to a blind person". Where would you start? How do you describe colors to someone who has never seen colors? To me, that would be a tremendous challenge.

Living with our grief may feel the same way...helpless. Certainly, there are typical and common grief responses like numbness, loss of concentration, mood changes, eating and sleeping patterns are changed, and we can lose complete control of our emotions in a heartbeat. All of these, and more, are very common grief responses.

The challenge is for us to give ourselves permission to grieve, and even permission to be different in our own grief journey. There are no "cookie-cutter grievers" where everyone is just alike.

We grieve according to our personality, the relationship we had with the person who died, the manner of their death, and even other losses in our life. So many unique factors are involved in the grief journey.

So yes, we can feel helpless dealing with grief. Personally, I believe it helps to put words to our grief feelings. To organize the grief feelings,

then express the feelings, that is
MOURNING. Everyone grieves, but not everyone
mourns in healthy ways.

 The organized and outward expression of grief can
soften the pain and intensity of the journey. Grief
will never go away, but it is possible to live in grief
and not feel helpless. It IS possible.

VISITING THE GRAVE

How often should a person visit a gravesite? That question has been asked many times. I always have the same answer, "as many times as you want to visit the gravesite...if ever".

A trip to the cemetery can be a very emotional and difficult time for some people. Seeing the grave, and the headstone, can create a struggle with accepting the reality of a death. Going to a cemetery should be an individual choice, and never anything forced upon a person.

Some are comfortable visiting the gravesite on a regular basis, everyone is different. Some have no plans or intentions of ever going there again. Either way is OK, whatever is right for each person.

Some use the occasion to honor the memory of a loved one by placing flowers on the grave. Others place small sculptures or decorations that are linked to memories. Flags are often placed upon the grave of a Veteran to honor their service to our country.

It can be very healthy to visit a grave and express any words that need to be said. Verbalizing feelings can give relief and soften the pain for some. It may be that a visit to the grave is the outlet needed to encourage mourning.

LIVING LIFE IN PENCIL

"Life should be lived in pencil...it changes"

For a dozen years in my early life I worked for home designers, architects, and engineers. I learned quickly to draw all plans in pencil, because there would always need to be changes to a design. From the early sketches to the final set of drawings, erasers were needed to make changes.

Life consists of changes. Some we control, some we try to avoid. Some changes will draw hearts together in close friendship, other changes will build walls between the best of friends.

The death of a loved one brings unbelievable changes into life. Schedules change, routines change, energy levels and sleep patterns change, focus changes, appetites change, and often friends change.

The most constant action after a loss is CHANGE. It never seems to end. Our goals and dreams change, our passion for life can change. In reality, we always expect changes in life and relationships...someday FAR into the future. But we are never prepared for the changes that follow a death.

Seek others who have experienced changes in life. Become part of a grief support group, or an online group. It helps to know others who have changes in life also. You are not alone.

Learn to take small steps in the grief journey. Give yourself permission to feel...and to change.

How has your experience changed you? Can you put it into words?

LET IT GO

Clara Barton was the founder of the American Red Cross. When a friend reminded her of an earlier vicious verbal attack on her by someone, she said, "I distinctly remember forgetting that". What an amazing attitude, to forgive and forget to the point that the incident no longer had any control over her. That is God's kind of forgiveness.

I know what forgiveness is in the Spiritual realm, God's forgiveness to me, and my forgiveness of others. I depend upon that each moment....every heartbeat.

But forgiveness in grief has a different definition. In the area of grief I believe forgiveness is "giving up the hope of a different or better yesterday". Something that was said or done 24 hours ago, or 24 years ago, will never be any different. It will always be the same, it will never change. Why hold onto it?

It is my choice to hold onto something from the past, or let it go where it belongs...in the past. Many people struggle today over something that occurred in the past. The only thing left is the "weight of unforgiveness", and that is a very heavy load for anyone to carry.

Giving up the hope of a different or better yesterday is not saying who is right or wrong, or accusing others. It is simply saying that we choose to no longer let the past control our present and our future. Why be miserable and shorten our own life and happiness by holding onto something from the past? Of course we will always remember what was said or done. But it is healthy to push it to the back of our mind and not focus on the hurt, bitterness, or resentment that can occur.

COINS ON GRAVES

"A Penny saved, is a penny earned" -Ben Franklin

For generations, visitors to Ben Franklin's gravesite in Pennsylvania developed a habit of tossing pennies onto his grave. Many have adopted this good luck tradition of tossing pennies onto the graves of their loved ones.

Many years ago I conducted a graveside service in an old cemetery. As I was leaving, I glanced down and noticed a penny on the ground. Not only was there a penny in the walkway, but the grave next to it was covered with pennies. There were countless pennies on top of the ground, and some almost covered with soil. It was as if entire handfuls of pennies were scattered across the entire grave. I had never seen that before, and have never seen it since.

When you see a coin on the grave of a serviceman or woman, it is a sign that another member of the military stopped to pay their respects. According to tradition, there is a meaning behind each type of coin:

- Penny: There is no formal relationship with the deceased, but it honors their service and their family
- Nickel: You trained in boot camp with the deceased

141

- Dime: You served with the deceased in some capacity in the military
- Quarter: You were with the deceased when he or she died

Leaving coins on a gravesite is a sign of respect for military members. It is symbolic that the deceased is still in the thoughts of others, and they also last longer than flowers.

This tradition has joined people together for centuries, it is a small reminder of the value of life…it is priceless. In some cultures, people will leave candles on the gravesite, some leave trinkets, crosses, stones, photographs, and especially flowers. All of these items, and many others, are symbolic of paying respect to the life and memory of loved ones. Leaving items on a gravesite is an example of mourning a loss, an outward expression of the grief.

THE BUST OF OPPORTUNITY

It was an ugly sculpture. I knew it, and it was obvious to anyone who saw it...it was ugly. But, the "message" of the sculpture, what it represented, was the most important part. This sculpture required me to explain the meaning, more than any other sculpture I have ever created.

I'll describe it to you. It was the bust of a man. He had a long shaggy beard, a long moustache that covered his mouth. His eyebrows were full, bushy, and hung over his eyes. His hair was long, unkept, and spread every direction.

Except from the ears back, across the entire back of his head...there was no hair, he was slick bald. All his hair was up front, none on the back of the head. Get the image?

This is the bust of "opportunity". All the hair is on the front, nothing is on the back. So, if we are going to catch hold of an opportunity, we must grab it up front while there is something to hold onto. Because once an opportunity gets past us, there is nothing to grab hold of.

Unfortunately, we recognize many opportunities from the backside. It is quite common to miss opportunities because we did not recognize them. Then, once it is past, we realize what we missed. Too late.

I am trying to recognize opportunities when they are in front of me, instead of looking at them from the backside after they have gone by. It will help our focus, and hopefully will allow us to enjoy more of the pleasures in life and relationships. Are you ready to grab the next opportunity?

SIT AND TALK AWHILE

Come here, let's sit awhile and talk...tell me about your day.

Has someone ever made that statement to you? To me, that statement indicates interest, respect, and a willingness to know more about the other person and their feelings. You are a blessed person if someone has actually given you the time to share and talk on the "feeling level" without any judgement.

Here is a little challenge, a little exercise in reviewing relationships. These relationships can be with someone we have known for years, or a new relationship we are just beginning to build.

If you could invite someone to come "sit awhile and talk" with you...who would it be? Make a list of 5 people you would enjoy talking to about life...any 5 people...alive or dead...family, friends, or historical figures.

Then, once your 5 are selected, what would be important to talk about with them? What would you like to hear from them? What would you like for them to hear from you?

Another interesting aspect of this exercise is that you can actually write down the subjects and questions you would have for each person. You will not be making up the responses, the questions are already with you…this just helps organize them for you.

I really hope someone makes that statement to you…."Come here, let's sit awhile and talk…tell me about your day".

BLINDFOLDS AND ROLLERCOASTERS

I have been guilty...I admit it. Many times over my years of working with grievers I have made the statement that "grief is like riding a rollercoaster of emotions". That is true in many ways because of the ups and downs, the sudden twists and turns.

But, grief is more like riding a rollercoaster with a blindfold covering your eyes. Can you imagine what that would be like? You would not be able to brace yourself for the next twist in the track because you did not see it coming, you could not take a deep breath when it suddenly dropped off into a quick turn. The turns can be sudden, and we cannot always recognize them.

You may be grocery shopping, on a very normal day. Suddenly you turn down an aisle and see someone who looks just like your loved one who died. Or, you see items on the shelf that you always purchased for them...their favorite food. Or, someone walks past you and their cologne or perfume was exactly the scent of your loved one. These are things that can happen suddenly, a *twist or turn in the grief* journey. They may be emotional, and no one understands their impact.

There are other differences related to the rollercoaster ride and grief. There are no screams of joy or excitement...these are replaced with sobs and

147

even outbursts of sorrow. There are no lines of people eager to take the next ride…we do not choose this path, this "ride" should never be a choice. No one can stop the ride so you can get off…you will never hear anyone say "that was fun, let's do it again".

So, I have learned to be cautious when I make the comparison of grief and a rollercoaster ride. I need to explain myself a little better.

REMEMBERING NAMES

John Partin and I attended a class together many years ago. Before the class started, John told me the speaker had been his college professor several years before but had lost contact. One thing John said was "he always amazed me with his ability to remember names of people".

Soon Dr. Leon Simpson walked into the room. He greeted many people as he entered. Then he walked straight toward us, reached out his hand and said, "Hello John Partin, it is great to see you again!". We were amazed he could remember John's name after so many years.

I spent time around Dr. Simpson for the next few years. I gained tremendous respect for him as a college president. But I was especially impressed with his ability to remember the names of people. He made others feel important, just by calling them by name several times during a conversation. Very impressive.

Names do not die with a loved one. A block of granite is nothing special...until the name of a loved one is etched into the stone. Then it becomes special. Let's look for ways to use the name of a loved one. Speak their name often, display objects that have their name visible. Some people may disagree with your actions, but that is their problem. How you choose to honor the name, and memory, of a loved one is your choice and your privilege. Look for new ideas to bring their name into the present. Their memory is here…why not use their name also? No excuses needed.

Names are important, let's use them.

DIFFERENT TYPES OF HUGS

Each day, I read the words and stories of many walking the grief journey. There is a common statement repeated over and over. "I miss their hugs". Hugging someone can be so normal and commonplace that it can be taken for granted…until they are gone.

Hugs come in different types. A "shoulder hug" may be the most accepted hug in society, making contact from the side of a person. We can "hug a neck" with others we feel close to, in a way to exhibit care and friendship. We can "hug a body" of those with whom we have built a level of trust and respect, an agreement from both parties involved.

But there is another hug I want to suggest. We can "hug the heart". Often this is the option that remains for us following a loss. But how do we "hug the heart" of someone who has died?

- Use their name in conversation. Names do not die, so continue to speak their name often, wear it on jewelry, tattoos, or clothing. Each time you use their name you are "hugging their heart".
- Tell stories about them. Surround yourself with people who will not only let you share your story but they will also add their stories of your loved one. There will be laughter and

tears. When you share stories, you are "hugging their heart".

- Intentionally play music they loved, wear clothing they loved, and display photos of them. Each act is a way to "hug their heart". I know it is not the same as in person, but our role now is to honor their life, to make sure they are never forgotten, to "hug their heart".

A HOLE IN THE WORLD

"Where you used to be, there is a hole in the world, which I find myself constantly walking around in the daytime, and falling in at night. I miss you like hell." - Edna St. Vincent Millay (American poet and playwright)

This quote by Edna St. Vincent Millay has always been one of my favorites…because it truthfully describes grief. She experienced a life of illness and loss; suffered a nervous breakdown; many of her friends died; and her husband died following a short illness. She knew grief.

During the daytime hours, we can stay busy with activities. There are usually people we can see, we can have social contact if we wish to, it is easier to "stay busy" in the daytime.

But at night…things can change. Millay refers to falling into a hole at night. That can be what grief feels like. The night can present loneliness, quietness, and reminders of a loss.

Intentionally make efforts to change this frequent occurrence. Instead of quietness…add music to the evening. Instead of being alone…call a friend who understands the need to be heard. Instead of reflecting upon things that "did not or cannot happen" because of a loss…dream and make plans to experience new things that "can happen". Set goals, small steps to a forward movement. Check the small steps off a list to show desired progress in a future, a plan, a dream to live in spite of the hole in the world. It is not possible to "fill the hole" left after a death, but it is possible to make plans to avoid falling into it on a regular basis.

You are not alone in this journey…an army of like minds and broken hearts can add support and guidance. Do not give up.

THEIR FAVORITES

I believe we need to seek a balance between the heavy weight of grief and turning our thoughts to a lighter side. Let's think about our favorites in life...I hope you join me by sharing your responses.

- What is your favorite color? (Blue)
- What is your favorite food? (Mexican)
- What is your favorite music? (Classic Country)
- What is your favorite therapy/escape? (sculpting)

This will be another reminder of how different we can be in many areas, and also how we can be drawn closer with things that are similar.

Think of the favorites of your loved one. Perhaps you knew them well enough to complete these same areas to honor their memory.

- What was their favorite color?
- What was their favorite food?
- What was their favorite music?
- What was their favorite therapy/escape?

Thank you for joining me in this little break from some heavy grief material. It is important to look for ways to balance emotions. I hope this little exercise provided a comfortable break for you.

TATTOOS

Tattooing is an art form of body modification where a pigment is inserted into a skin to change it's color permanently. It is a very old tradition and today is more popular and socially acceptable than ever. It has become so mainstream that even Mattel started selling Barbie dolls with tattoos. People of both sexes, of all economic classes, and of all ages wear tattoos if they want to. Today, at least one fifth of adults in the United States has at least one tattoo. (historyoftattoos.net (2022).

After a loss, many people get tattoos in honor of their loved one. It seems any design is possible thanks to advancements in technology, tools, and methods. It is common to have tattoos on the body of photos, butterflies, signatures, and even the handwriting of a loved one who has died. Body parts from fingers to toes, ankles to wrists, arms to legs, chests, shoulders, ear lobes and beyond can be adorned with artwork to honor a special person.

Personally, I am not comfortable with needles and putting dye under my skin. I admire and respect those who choose this manner of honoring a loved one. Some of the tattoos I've seen are very creative and artistic. These are permanent ways to carry the presence of a loved one.

People leave a permanent impression upon our life and heart, much like tattoos do for the skin. These impressions will never fade away, and they can never be removed. Because of our love and commitments in relationships, we are "marked for life". We will always carry a "heart tattoo" with us.

THE RELUCTANT CAREGIVER

Several years ago I was having lunch with a lady who was the caregiver for her husband who had Alzheimer's. She talked of his changing health, and how it involved both mental and physical changes. This was a story I had heard many times before from women and men caring for a family member.

But then she made a statement that got my attention, and caught me off guard. She said, "You need to write a book on the reluctant caregiver. I am the sole caregiver for a man I do not even like! He has put me through Hell during our marriage, now I am expected by everyone to be his caregiver".

A reluctant caregiver. These are not words that are expressed very often. The normal caregiver situation usually involves a family member or friend who is extremely dedicated to another person, and someone who tirelessly remains committed to the difficult task.

No one on the "outside" can know the history of another individual or couple. The family dynamics can be covered up and never made public.

Reluctant caregivers must provide care in spite of their feelings toward the patient. They may put up a

158

good front for others to see, but the real situation may never be known by others.

The grief experience of a reluctant caregiver may be complicated due to regrets and guilt. Both of these responses are normal following a loss. It helps to find a safe person who will allow the feelings to be expressed with no judgement.

If this describes your situation, do not give up. You are not alone. Do not give up.

DEALING WITH THE FIRSTS

It is impossible to do anything for the 1st time...again! We only get one chance to do something for the first time, only one time. Life is full of "first time events" from birth to death.

Reviewing a relationship is very normal after a death. We search for those highlights in our memories, those feel good times we enjoyed with someone.

I remember from my early school years the teachers gave out little "gold stars" for a report card that had good grades. Those "gold stars" were reason to be proud. There are "gold star moments" in relationships. Those are the events we look back upon and think "I'm so glad that happened".

Relationships consist of 3 parts: In the BEGINNING, there will be many "firsts" as the relationship develops and grows.

Then there are memories that FEEL GOOD. Those are the gold star moments, great memories. They are special to remember, in fact, it would be helpful to write them down as they cross your mind.

Relationships may also have things that HURT. These may be at the end of relationship if you saw a loved one suffer. These are things you wished had never happened. But they did. There are usually far more things that FEEL GOOD than things that HURT. But it is normal to have both in a relationship.

Grievers are facing many "firsts" without the person they loved. They face things that they did not choose. These "firsts" can be painful, devastating, and can produce a multitude of emotions. Don't give up. Keep moving through the "firsts" in the grief journey.

STACKING STONES

Stacking stones has been part of human culture for thousands of years. Around the world, the custom of stacking stones is common for personal meditation time, with each stone symbolic of a prayer. The Bible records the stacking of stones following a miracle, and to put in place the opportunity for sharing the story behind them. When someone asked "What do these stones mean?", it paved the way for the story to be repeated, over and over again, for generations.

If you were going to stack stones for remembrance, think of all the places you would need to go. Would there be a stack of stones to designate the place where you first met your loved one? How about a stack of stones that marked a place that holds fun and happy memories? Would there also be a stack of stones at that private escape or getaway location?   Perhaps stacks of stones would be needed at the location of a proposal? A wedding? A birth? A graduation? Think of all the places stones could be stacked that would invite the conversation with "What do these stones mean?"

Stacks of stones were early grave markers when a loved one was buried. Not only did it mark an important place on the face of the earth, but it would also lead someone to ask "What do these stones mean"? The symbolic stacking of stones could be added to a garden area of your home. The stones could be a constant reminder of the impact of a loved one, a reminder that we were blessed, and we were changed. It would provide an opportunity for someone to ask "What do these stones mean"?

TYING RIBBONS TO REMEMBER

Unfortunately, an accident in our city took the life of a young police officer. This tragedy shook our city, and led to public displays of support for the family he leaves behind, and for the entire police department.

As I drove through town recently, I noticed hundreds of blue ribbons tied to trees, light posts, street signs, and buildings. These blue ribbons are outward expressions of support, a visible reminder that this officer is missed and will always be remembered in this community.

One tradition of tying ribbons to trees can be traced to messages given to soldiers returning from the Civil War. The message was that they have been missed and someone is welcoming them home. There are several other stories of it's beginning, and even a popular song in the 1970's reinforced the practice of tying ribbons to trees. Regardless of the beginnings, we notice these outward expressions of support, and the longing for someone's presence.

If you were to tie a ribbon onto a tree to honor a loved one...what color would you select? Was it their favorite color? It would be OK to tie a ribbon in their honor on special days of remembrance, it is an outward expression of feelings.

Remember, our grief is a confusing mass of emotions bottled up within us. Mourning is when we put words and actions to these feelings and express them. When "grief goes public", even as simple as tying a ribbon, it becomes mourning. It is very healthy to mourn, to express our feelings. Perhaps tying ribbons is a good healing process for you.

NEVER GET OVER IT

"To anyone who needs to hear it: We don't "get over" or "move on" from our trauma. We are forced to make space for it. We carry it. We learn to live with it. And, sometimes we thrive in spite of it" -unknown

We "get over" the common cold in a few days or a week. Our immune system is structured by God to fight it off and provide recovery over a period of time. We can all attest to the fact that we "got over it", when we talk of the common cold.

But, grief is not the same. We do not "get over it". Some very insensitive people may even imply or voice the statement that you should just "get over it".

Grief turns our world upside down, we are in shock, we are numb, our life has changed forever. We have lost the physical relationship with someone we loved deeply. They will never be present in our life again. How can we possibly "get over it"?

Some will even state that we need to "move on" in life. What does that even mean? What does it look like to "move on"? I read an illustration recently that grief is like having a broken leg. Over time there may be a sense of healing and recovery. But we will always walk with a limp! Perhaps it has been years since the death occurred, but there will be times we will "limp" emotionally because of the changes to our life. Emotionally and spiritually we will never lose loved ones who die…we lose the physical relationship.

Do not try to "get over it". Do not attempt to "move on". We will learn to live as a griever, and it is not always pretty. There will be good moments and there will be bad moments. But we will always be grievers.

MOURNING NOTES:

MOURNING NOTES:

TOOLS

LISTENING OR HEARING?

He was only 17 years old, but I learned a very valuable lesson from him. He was attending a grief support group I was leading because his friend had died.

As part of my usual presentation, I made the statement that "we all need someone to listen to us". I had made that statement in grief groups for almost 2 decades…but this time it changed.

He said, "That is right Bob, we all need someone who will listen to us…but we also need someone who will hear us". He was absolutely right.

Some people will LISTEN to us, the words may go in 1 ear and out the other ear…but they listened. As grievers we need someone who will HEAR us. These special folks will HEAR the words and feelings of our heart. In order to spell the word "heart", you must first spell the word "hear", then add a "t".

Pay special attention to that person who "HEARS you". They will listen to your words, but they also hear what is not being said. They will have a way to relate to the grief and feel the pain of the heart. These people can be trusted to guide you into the journey of grief, they will help find the times of comfort.

WHEN WILL I FEEL BETTER?

"Patience is not the ability to wait, but the ability to keep a good attitude while waiting" – unknown

Some people are better at waiting than others. But, the grief process cannot be hurried or put on a fast track to a completion. A few weeks may seem like a year, and a year may seem like only a few weeks. The time factor makes no sense anymore, everything is wrong and feels a little bit off balance following a loss.

The most common question I receive from a griever is "When will I feel better?". That is a very good question, because everyone wants to feel better. We want the pain to soften or go away. Patience usually is pretty thin during this time.

There is an answer to the "when will I feel better" question. The answer? When your grief becomes mourning you will feel better.

Grief is on the inside following a loss. It is a bundle of painful emotions and confusing facts. Grief is emotionally heavy. Grief will change our ability to think, move, and respond to our surroundings. We are numb and lose the ability to concentrate.

Mourning is the outward expression of grief through words or actions. It is "grief gone public". Mourning may be tears or screams, it may be organized or erratic. Telling our story is mourning, it is putting words to the grief.

"Blessed are those who MOURN, for they shall be comforted" (Matthew 5:4). When will we feel better? The Bible says we feel better when our grief becomes mourning.

THE TOOLS

In life, we get out of something what we put into it. We will get out of these tools just what we put into them. We will identify our grief, organize it, and learn tools to express it to soften the pain of loss.

Everyone is at a different place in their grief, so I do not want anyone to feel pressure when looking at these materials. Just absorb what you can absorb, and do what you can at this time in your grief journey.

I am responsible TO you, but I am not responsible FOR you. If I was responsible FOR you folks I could not sleep at night, I would worry about you all the time. My responsibility is to provide the very best grief materials I know about. I can do that, and I will do that. What you do with these materials is your choice and responsibility.

NORMAL RESPONSES TO GRIEF

This is not a checklist where you need to achieve each one. But do not be surprised if you can identify with some of these responses:

* Numb to people and events around you....feeling out of place....living in a "fog". Some refer to this as "grief brain".

* A feeling of tightness in the throat or heaviness in the chest. Grief impacts us physically...self-care during this time is vital.

* A feeling of emptiness in the stomach and a change in eating habits. You may lose interest in food...or you may eat all the time. You may see a pattern of snacking your way through the day instead of eating healthy meals.

* Feelings of restlessness, losing the ability to focus and concentrate. The brain is in shock...it does not function properly. You may forget names, dates, and easily misplace things. While driving, you may miss turns, get lost, or even have an accident. Please use caution when driving. Intentionally focus.

* Sensing the presence of your loved one around you. You may think you hear their voice, or even see

their face in a crowd. Remember, we lose people physically, but emotionally and spiritually we never lose them.

* Wandering aimlessly and forgetting to finish projects. You may have several projects started and move to another one before finishing the first one.

* Sleeping patterns change. Either we sleep constantly or we cannot sleep at all. Many enter a pattern of napping through the day and night, and not able to get a restful night of sleep.

* Experience a preoccupation with memories of your loved one. Memories are very special. Keep a journal of memories...they are yours, no one has the same memories.

* Feelings of guilt or regret over things that did or did not happen in the relationship.

* Feelings of intense anger at the loved one for leaving.

* Feeling abandoned by the loved one. We must realize that relationships end before we are through with them.

* Feeling a need to protect others by not talking about the loss. This is usually to protect children. In reality, the best thing to do is talk with them about memories.

* Needing to tell, retell, and remember stories of the loved one and the experience of their death. The more we tell the story the more real it becomes.

* Mood changes over the slightest things, having some good days and some bad days. Actually we have good moments and bad moments.

* Tears at UNEXPECTED times. You do not want to cry in the grocery store...or while driving...or while enjoying a pretty day...but you will. Memories can sneak up on us and bring tears...anywhere. No need to apologize...this is very common.

SECONDARY LOSSES

Have you ever thrown a stone into a pool of still water? If so, you can recall how the stone disappeared. But from the point it contacted the surface of the water there were circular ripples extending outward from the center. These ripples would have never appeared if the stone had not interrupted the calmness of the water.

This is a picture of the grief process and the subsequent reminders of a loss. When the loss occurred, the "stone" entered into the calm of your life. The impact of a stone into the water seems to create a hole that is quickly covered up by the ripples.

The impact of your loss can make it feel like a hole in your heart, only to have ripples of pain overwhelm your peace. These ripples are "SECONDARY LOSSES". They may be produced by the awareness of birthdates, holidays, anniversaries, seeing a photograph of a loved one, or even hearing a favorite song. These, and many other reminders, make us aware of many "SECONDARY LOSSES" connected to our primary loss.

You may experience the LOSS OF JOY: When faced with the reality of a loved one's death, we seem to lose the joy and laugher once experienced

178

with them. Joy can disappear and leave behind a painful silence. We wonder if we will ever experience joy and laughter again in our life. Our reason for joy has died.

The LOSS OF BALANCE is very real. The support and encouragement we receive from others can provide the balance to assure our stability in life. Emotional balance can be the hug without words, the nod of support and encouragement, someone to serve as our emotional compass.

In one sense, we have lost that person who always walked beside us and provided the balance in life when we needed it. Not only was this a physical support, but emotional support also. Having that person we could share our heart with provided a sense of balance from within. When this changes, there is a deep void.

LOSS OF DREAMS is often overlooked. Relationships end before we are through with them. There can be a feeling of being cheated or robbed when a relationship ends. Dreaming again can be difficult, and it may take time to develop. These lost dreams are usually expressed with the words…"we always planned to….." . What is your response?

The LOSS OF INTIMACY is often overlooked in the grief process. The loss of the physical aspect of a relationship, the intimacy that formed a bond of trust, can be a tremendous loss. This emptiness, this void, is intensified with the realization that the person you have given yourself to totally is no longer present with you. In many ways, it is an unspoken loss. It has been such a private area in the relationship that it is difficult to discuss. But, it is real.

The LOSS OF SUPPORT is when we lose that person we thought we could rely upon, someone we thought we could draw strength from, someone who could provide a sense of safety. When that person is gone, there can be a sense of being vulnerable and helpless. It is not easy to find support. There needs to be the element of trust before we lean on someone for support. It can take time, but is worth the effort.

The LOSS OF SECURITY can be present at many levels. Physical security might involve having someone's presence and protection; financial security can be the assurance of assets and being financially comfortable in life; emotional security can be having a safe person we can share everything with. The loss, or change, in any of these areas can intensify the grief process.

There can be a LOSS OF SELF ESTEEM because we often draw it from others who instill worth and value into our life. If that person is gone, our worth and value can be impacted. The challenge is to believe in our own abilities, even though no one is there to affirm us.

Grief can paralyze us emotionally, and we may have a LOSS OF MOTIVATION. Our desire to return to a normal or routine schedule will be absent. It's common to pull into a shell, avoiding people and responsibilities. There can be a complete lack of interest in anything, even those things that we enjoyed before the loss.

Because grief is exhausting work, we may experience the LOSS OF ENERGY. It is hard work...and it is heart work. Your physical and emotional energy levels can be drained. You might feel empty. It is difficult to provide support to others when you are emotionally drained. It requires focusing on self care.

There can be entire books written on LOSS OF PURPOSE in grief. Perhaps you were an excellent caregiver for your loved one. You did a great job of providing for them physically and emotionally. Now that death has occurred...what do you do now? It's like being great at your job, and then suddenly you are unemployed. Where do you go from here?

The LOSS OF UNCONDITIONAL LOVE is powerful. You may have lost the only person who has ever loved you unconditionally. Unconditional love says, "I love you…regardless…period". It does not say "I will love you IF, or I will love you WHEN". It is never critical or judgmental. This is a tremendous loss. We do not just go to the corner and find someone who will love us in this manner. Unconditional love is built on trust, respect, and wanting the best for another person.

The LOSS OF FUTURE can be overwhelming. When a loss occurs, it is very difficult to look into the future. It's difficult to make long term plans while surviving moment to moment. Futures plans involved the presence of a loved one who is no longer available. There will be times to re-dream, to make long term plans. These plans will be different because all areas of life are different now.

The LOSS OF A SAFE PERSON leaves a big hole in our life. There are times we need a safe person in our life. They are the unique person who will lend us their ears, and not just their mouth. We confide in them, share hurts and secrets with them, knowing it is safe for eternity. When that person dies, we have a deep sense of being abandoned, and our safe outlet is not available. It takes time to develop a safe person relationship. Give yourself that time.

The LOSS OF A BEST FRIEND is losing that person who knows, and accepts, the "real us". We need someone who is comfortable with our laughter and our tears. When this person dies, or the relationship changes, our walls of safety might go up to provide security for our heart.

The LOSS OF A CHEERLEADER is perhaps the most overlooked SECONDARY LOSS. When we face challenges or struggles in life, we need someone who really believes in us, someone who encourages us. We need a CHEERLEADER. Someone in that role can provide the support and strength for us to achieve our greatest potential. When that person dies, we may question our ability to meet the challenges in life. We miss the person who encouraged us when we had doubts. Be open to another cheerleader, someone who steps up to believe in you.

So, as we can tell by reading the previous articles, the LOSS OF NORMAL is a secondary loss. What was once normal will never be normal again. There will be a new normal, but it will be different. Living your life without the presence of your loved one will never feel normal. Now it is normal to feel the emptiness, the loneliness, and the awareness that part of your heart is missing.

HONORING RELATIONSHIPS

Relationships end before we are through with them.

Recently I have used the phrase "softening the pain" of grief. Since it is impossible to take the pain away, I believe there are ways to soften the pain. Here is a beginning exercise that will guide broken hearts.

What is the earliest memory of your loved one? When did the relationship begin? Do you recall the starting point of the relationship? What feeling words could you use to describe that beginning?

Next, can you name some high points and positive times in the relationship? These will be the life events you are so glad to have in your memory bank. List as many of these "feel good moments" as you can.

Then, identify anything in the relationship that hurts. This might bring negative memories to your mind, but all relationships have these 3 elements: a starting point, things that feel good, and things that hurt. Most relationships will have far more things that feel good than those that hurt.

This exercise helps put the relationship in proper perspective. Often after a death we focus on the last days, the last words, the last breath, etc. But in reality, there IS more to the relationship than the end of one. Let's identify some of these elements that made up the relationship.

WRITING TO SOFTEN THE PAIN

Often in life we are so busy we do not take time to say things we intend to say. If death occurs before we express those things there can be a feeling of helplessness. What can we do with those thoughts now? They still need to be verbalized and expressed. This series of "softening the pain" sentences presents the opportunity to put words to grief. If there is unfinished business in the relationship, if there are regrets or guilt, hurts, apologies, or even expressions of gratitude...these "tools" can guide the process of putting words to the grief so it can be expressed. The process of putting words to feelings is where MOURNING occurs...the outward expression of grief.

The material below is the "heart" of this grief method to put words to the grief so it becomes MOURNING. Grief is what we feel on the inside, MOURNING is when our grief is expressed. We find comfort when we mourn...not when we grieve.

Imagine you had the opportunity to talk with your loved one again. Complete these sentences to share the thoughts and feelings that are important to you. Express everything that is on your heart to say with each sentence.

MOURNING MOMENTS

- I want to thank you for…

- My fondest memory of you is…

- I want to apologize to you for…

- I forgive you for…

- It feels GOOD when I think of…

- It HURTS when I think of…

- It makes me ANGRY when I think of…

- I feel GUILTY when I think of…

- I wish I had…

- Something I always wanted to tell you was…

- I would like to have heard you say…

- I want you to know…

UNFINISHED BUSINESS

"Unfinished business" is a term commonly used to describe things left unsaid or undone after a death. Because schedules and opportunities do not always allow for time to share personally, it can leave feelings behind that the relationship is not finished, not complete. You may still have things you wanted to say to them.

Imagine you could talk with your loved one again, imagine you could say what you need to say in these areas:

- "Something I always wanted to tell you….."
  We may always think we have tomorrow to say what is on our mind and in our heart. But death does not care, it can come unexpectedly. What has been on your heart to share with them?

- "I would like to have heard you say…". Grief is not always what we say or what we do. Often we grieve what we did not hear from someone before they died. What do you need to hear from them? Can you put words to what you need to hear?

- "I want you to know…" This is the opportunity to express any of the grief feelings that did not seem to fit into any of the previous statements. This area can contain statements on any aspect of the relationship…any unfinished business. Now is the time to express it.

This can be a very emotional exercise. It is healthy to identify grief, organize grief, and express grief. Then it becomes mourning.

FORGIVENESS

In the process to ORGANIZE the emotions of our grief, we must confront some areas that are not always comfortable for us. This may be one of those areas:

- "If I could talk with you again…something I need to say is that I FORGIVE YOU FOR _____."

This may be a very difficult area, but it is necessary in order to find peace with any unfinished business. This forgiveness if not saying who was right or wrong, but it IS saying that the area of conflict needs to be put in the past.

A good definition of forgiveness is "giving up the hope of a different yesterday". Things that were said or done, whether 24 hours ago or 24 years ago, will never be any different than the moment they happened. Our choice is to hang onto the feelings of resentment, bitterness, and unforgiveness…or, we can choose to say goodbye to those feelings and let them be in the past where they belong.

Life is too short and fragile to allow past conflicts to dictate our attitude today. Dwelling on the conflict but never taking steps to resolve it is keeping the pain alive. We forgive others for OUR sake, not for their sake. Forgiveness can lead to our peace, regardless of the response of the other person.

Yesterday can never be any different. We cannot change yesterday, but we can certainly mess up today by trying. Give up the hope of it ever being any different. Doing so can bring peace and acceptance to a very important area of the grief journey.

GUILT AND REGRETS

This article considers the difference between "GUILT" and "REGRET".

We may have "GUILT" if we made an intentional decision and we knew what the outcome would be. Key words: "INTENTIONAL DECISION" and "WE KNEW". Guilt can become a very heavy load, especially after the death of a loved one. You may question what you can do with the feelings of guilt now that your loved one is not available for a conversation.

REGRET is quite common after a death. Often we are so busy in the caregiving role, or just busy with life, we fail to take time and say important things. After the death, we may say "I wish I had....". Those are the feelings of regrets.

I want to encourage you to write responses to these statements. It can be 1 word or 5 pages, you are the only one to know when you are finished. This is an important step to identify unfinished business, organize it, and express it. Imagine you could talk with them again, what would you say in response to these statements?

- "I feel guilty when I think of..."

- "I wish I had...."

"THE STORY BEHIND THE HEALING HEART"

"Can you make a sculpture from a photograph?" I turned to face the person who spoke these words and looked into the faces of a 3 generational family. As we spoke, one of the women opened an envelope and began spreading the photos of a young boy across the table in front of me.

"Could you take some photos from the side so I can have a profile view?" I asked. The woman quickly uttered a statement that had probably been rehearsed a hundred times in her mind. "This is our 3 ½ year old grandson. He drowned 2 weeks ago in our backyard." Tears streamed down her face as she said, "We were in your gallery last month and Malachi was with us. After his funeral my husband said we should come see if you could sculpt a bust of Malachi."

She shared that they were having a very difficult time, they loved Malachi so very deeply. I heard how their faith in God was supporting them, how they were finding strength in His presence each day, and in one another. There had been many heartaches in their lives, but nothing had broken their hearts like the drowning death of Malachi.

During the process of sculpting the bust of Malachi, the Lord inspired me to sculpt the HEALING HEART. Psalms 147:3 says "HE heals the brokenhearted, HE binds up their wounds". The HEALING HEART has <u>scars</u> upon it to represent past losses that have healed. This family had suffered many other losses over the years. The HEALING HEART has a <u>break</u> to symbolize a tragic event that breaks the heart. Malachi's death was the event that broke the hearts in this family. The HEALING HEART has a <u>bandage</u> placed over the break to represent the person who kept you from 'falling apart" during your time of loss…your "<u>bandage</u>". Family and friends had provided support and comfort for this family during this tragedy….they served as a "bandage" for their broken heart. Bandages do not heal, they just hold us together while God does His healing.

We need people in our life who help "hold us together" when we feel like falling apart. Can you identify these people? They cannot heal a broken heart, but they can provide comfort and support when needed.

"FOOTPRINTS IN THE SAND"

"Footprints in the Sand" was a popular poem written in 1964 by Margaret Fishback Powers. Her poem has become popular on cards, books, jewelry, and clothing. The words in this poem have encouraged generations with the mental picture of God carrying us during times of trials. It is then, when there is only 1 set of "footprints in the sand", that HE carries us.

Have you ever thought of the "footprints" that your loved one has left behind? If you could retrace their steps through life, we could only imagine the impact upon others.

It is very possible, that as you look back over your lives together, there could be some difficult parts of the journey. Life is not always roses and sunshine, there can be some days that are dark and devastating.

Think back over your life. Was there someone who "carried you" during those difficult days? Would it be the footprints of a parent? A spouse? A child? A friend? I believe a loving God will provide people to support, guide, and carry us during the times of trials. Who was that person for you? Whose "footprints" can you see in your life, the person God used to help "carry you?".

Do you realize we each may have the opportunity to support and "carry" another person? Instead of turning our back on someone who needs a friend during a crisis, perhaps we have been prepared to be there for them. Let's be sensitive to those needing to be carried. Let's be prepared to leave our "footprints in the sand" as we are used by God to help carry them.

"WASH DAY GRIEF"

Have you ever looked at the settings on your washing machine as they relate to grief? Consider these common washing machine settings:

 NORMAL: Normal responses following a loss may include mood changes, changes in eating and sleeping patterns, feelings of anger, abandonment, despair, loss of concentration, loss of energy, and the loss of motivation. These responses can vary based upon previous loss experiences, our relationships, and even our personality.

 SMALL LOAD: Each person's grief is a major life event. However, there may be some days the grief pain is not as intense. These days offer the time to catch your breath. Regardless of the relationship...regardless of the circumstances surrounding the loss...it is a major loss.

 LARGE LOAD: Grief can bring on very intense feelings. These feelings can be overwhelming, even to someone with a history of always being under control. We can be paralyzed emotionally because of the shock a loss brings.

 SPIN CYCLE: Several events can throw a griever into a "spin cycle". Holidays, birthdays, anniversaries, photos, music, food, and even fragrances can begin the "spin cycle" of emotions. These are normal twists and turns along the journey of grief.

 RINSE CYCLE: The rinse cycle is a time of refreshing. Tears provide a natural rinsing, a cleansing of the soul. Grief encompasses all of the confusing and painful emotions felt after a loss. Mourning is the outward expression of these feelings...whether through tears, words, or actions.

 COOL DOWN: No one can take grief away. Expressing grief to a safe person, or becoming part of a grief support group, can provide a "cool down" time. These steps can help soften the pain of grief, but the awareness of the loss will remain.

  Give yourself permission to be a "**NORMAL**" griever. Some days will bring a "**SMALL LOAD**" of grief...other days will consist of a "**LARGE LOAD**". The "**SPIN CYCLE**" may be intense at times...while the "**RINSE CYCLE**" of tears can cleanse the soul as we mourn the loss. Peace and acceptance can offer a "**COOL DOWN**" phase...a time of rest.

"THE WRAPPER"

A fatal heart attack had suddenly removed a man from the family circle. A few days after his funeral I met with the family for a time of remembrance. His daughter-in-law shared this with me.

Her 4 year old son asked "Where is grandpa now?". She told him "Grandpa is in Heaven now". The little boy smiled big and quietly went to bed. The next morning the family drove to the cemetery to see the grave. The young boy ran to the grave and saw it covered with flowers. He turned to his mom and asked, "Mommy, is THIS Heaven?".

That night as she put her son to bed, she removed a candy bar from her pocket. She tore open the wrapper, gave him some candy, and said "Let's talk about grandpa. What do you remember about grandpa?".

He told how grandpa had taken him fishing, they played ball, they went to the zoo together, grandpa had fixed his toys, and many other special memories.

When he finished the memories, and they finished the candy bar, mom slipped in bed beside him and held him very close. She said "Honey, grandpa is a lot like this candy bar. That good and delicious part of grandpa, the memories you just told me about...that is the part of grandpa that has gone to

Heaven. We can always talk about those good memories of grandpa."

Then she held up the wrapper of the candy bar and said "This is the part of grandpa we buried under those flowers at his grave...just grandpa's WRAPPER!"

The little boy quickly understood that we lose the physical part of people, but we can always talk about our sweet memories of them.

MOURNING NOTES:

MOURNING NOTES:

HOLIDAYS

HOLIDAYS AND SPECIAL DAYS

There are a total of 11 Federal holidays each year in the USA. Each of these holidays can have family rituals, reunions, and time for family/friends to gather. Of course, following a loss, these holidays can be very emotional instead of an uplifting time. It is common to try and avoid attending these gatherings because of the emotions they could stir.

Birthdays and anniversaries happen each day for someone. The pain of not having a loved one to help celebrate a joyous occasion can be very real. This often leads to time being spent alone, and can flow into a time of depression.

Here are some tips for celebrating these special days:

- Have a birthday party to honor a loved one. Invite family and friends, share memories, photos, music, and enjoy their favorite foods.
- Place stepping stones in a flower garden with their name inscribed into it
- Plant a tree in memory of your loved one
- Plan a butterfly release as a symbol of releasing hope and joy into the world as you remember your loved one
- Donate money in their name to an organization that provides counseling to

couples, or another organization that relates to their interests

As mentioned before, it is important to take the initiative in honoring someone. It must be intentional and planned. You may want to involve others, or you may be most comfortable with a private memory effort.

I believe you will be satisfied that the effort was made. Their memory deserves it.

COPING WITH HOLIDAYS

In a grief support group before the holidays several years ago, we discussed ways to cope with grief. Several mentioned taking a trip for a change in traditions and scenery. Two of the ladies announced to the group they would be taking a Christmas cruise to the West Indies.

About a week after Christmas I received a phone call from one of the ladies. She said, "Bob, I was miserable in paradise. I took my memories with me"! The getaway was not what she expected. There were constant reminders that her husband was no longer available to share life with her. It was a very painful experience.

It is true, a change in location for the holidays can help some people deal with their grief. But,it is impossible to leave memories at home. The emotions of grief can be stirred regardless of the location. It is not possible to "flip a switch" and turn grief off. It cannot be put in a suitcase and stored away.

Watching other couples having fun, hearing laughter and being around a festive environment was not relaxing for this lady. If you choose to plan a holiday trip…be aware…grief goes with you.

Develop an "emotional escape plan". Inform those you are with that you may need to spend time alone to gather emotions. Rejoin the group to experience new adventures in "doses" if needed, a little at a time. It is necessary to find the balance of grief emotions and new traditions. Just be aware.

HOLIDAYS

Thanksgiving. What are you thankful for? I believe we can look at all stages of life and identify things we are thankful for. Will you take time to do this?

From our childhood years…what are you most thankful for? Do you have a favorite childhood memory that is evidence of your thankfulness?

During the "growing up years" there can be times of thankfulness that are often overlooked. Who were you thankful for during those years when you were making the transition from a child to a young adult? Who was there for you during the good and bad times?

There will be adults who influenced us a young person, or even as an adult. Who are you thankful for because of the spiritual impact upon your life? Who provided insight and guidance in developing the life skills that you have today? Was there someone who provided the emotional stability you needed during that time?

It is good to stop and be thankful for those who influenced our lives. If possible, it is good to express your thankfulness to them. Just pausing to think about the blessings in our lifetime, taking time to be thankful for others, can add value to our life.

HONOR DAY

3:30AM…my mind woke up and would not go back to sleep. So, I got out of bed, fixed a cup of coffee, and began my day…earlier than usual. I want to share what my waking thought was…and I will also ask for your input and suggestions on this subject.

Everyone has a date we honor their birth…their birthday. Some are celebrated more than others as milestones in the journey of life. After a death, these birthdays can be difficult, awkward, and very emotional. I have an idea.

Let's develop "Honor Day". This can be a day set aside to intentionally honor the life of someone who has died. It can be held on any day, in any location, and in any manner that honors their life. Use your imagination, think outside the typical "grief box", consider these possibilities:

- Gather family and friends to the "Honor Day"
- Print t-shirts with photos to honor the person
- Suggest everyone wear a particular color because the person being honored loved that color
- Serve their favorite food, play their favorite music, and display photos of them

- Donations can be received and given to a cause the honored person believed in supporting
- Have a time when memories are shared on this "Honor Day"
- Expect a mixture of tears and laughter, after all…life consists of tears and laughter, they are normal expressions of life

What would you do to honor a life on "Honor Day". Perhaps we can soften the impact of their birthday, simply by making it an "Honor Day". Maybe, just maybe, a new tradition will begin.

HOLIDAY BLUES

Although the holidays are supposed to be a time of joy, good cheer, and high hopes for the New Year, many people experience seasonal "blues". These seasonal "blues" can be caused by increased stress and fatigue, unrealistic expectations, over commercialization of holidays, and the inability to be with family members.

Of course, the death of a loved one will make the holidays extremely difficult and intensely painful. Everything changes, normal disappears. Others may want to celebrate the holidays, but it is difficult to get into the holiday mood when dealing with grief.

Here are some ideas to help with the holiday "blues".

- Keep expectations manageable
- Be realistic about what you can and cannot do
- Give yourself permission to feel lonely or sad at times
- Volunteer to help someone less fortunate
- Don't be afraid to try something new
- Spend time with people who are supportive and care about you.
- Make time for yourself; be selfish, don't spend all your time providing for family and friends

- Create a peaceful place of refuge…a place you can retreat to if stress gets too heavy. Use books, music, or writing to give comfort.

The greatest gift you can give yourself is permission to care for yourself. It is an investment in yourself during the difficult grief journey.

GIFT CARDS

Someone had a brilliant idea! In practically any store, usually near the check-out section, there will be a display of gift cards. These gift cards can be purchased in various amounts, they can be used for such things as food, gasoline, books, music, etc. It can provide the practical option for shoppers.

I have never met anyone who turned down a gift card. They are very easy to purchase, they can be used online, the amounts can vary, and they can be used to meet personal choices.

A suggestion? Do your Christmas shopping at the gift card section! Write a personal note in a card to share how shopping would be too difficult this year, there have been many changes, then enclose a gift card selected for each person. It is OK. Going shopping in crowded malls and stores can be overwhelming for some people. Just hearing the festive music and seeing families together can be too much. This year, change your traditions and your "normal" way of expressing love and appreciation.

It is time to be "selfish". Take care of yourself during the holidays, it is a wise investment and will be worth the effort.

Think about it. One stop in one store and your entire task of shopping for others can be completed. Plan a "Gift Card Christmas". Make no apologies, those who care about your emotions will understand and respect your choice (and those who do not understand do not deserve a card...lol).

MOURNING NOTES:

MOURNING NOTES:

CONCLUSION

We will always be grievers. The purpose of these
MOURNING MOMENT articles is to soften the
grief pain a little bit. Perhaps as the pain of grief
softens, we will see that our grief does not need to
constantly overwhelm our life.

As we learn to mourn, to express the grief
outwardly, we will find moments of comfort in this
life-long journey.

"Blessed are those who MOURN, for they shall be
comforted" (Jesus, Matthew 5:4)

Bob Willis

Bob is a grief specialist who works with broken hearts. Since 1995 his passion has been to provide guidance and "tools" to grievers.

As an accomplished sculptor, Bob has designed many products that reflect empty and broken hearts as a result of the grief experience. Often, Bob will blend sculpting in clay into his grief presentations to illustrate the ever changing journey of grief and loss.

One of his most popular sculptures is a heart with stitches on it to symbolize past losses. A break down the middle of the heart represents a death or loss. Across the break is a bandage. Bandages do not heal, they just hold us together while God is doing the healing. Every griever needs a bandage.

Bob Willis

Rwillis14@cox.net

405-808-6925

Printed in Great Britain
by Amazon

15218180R00129